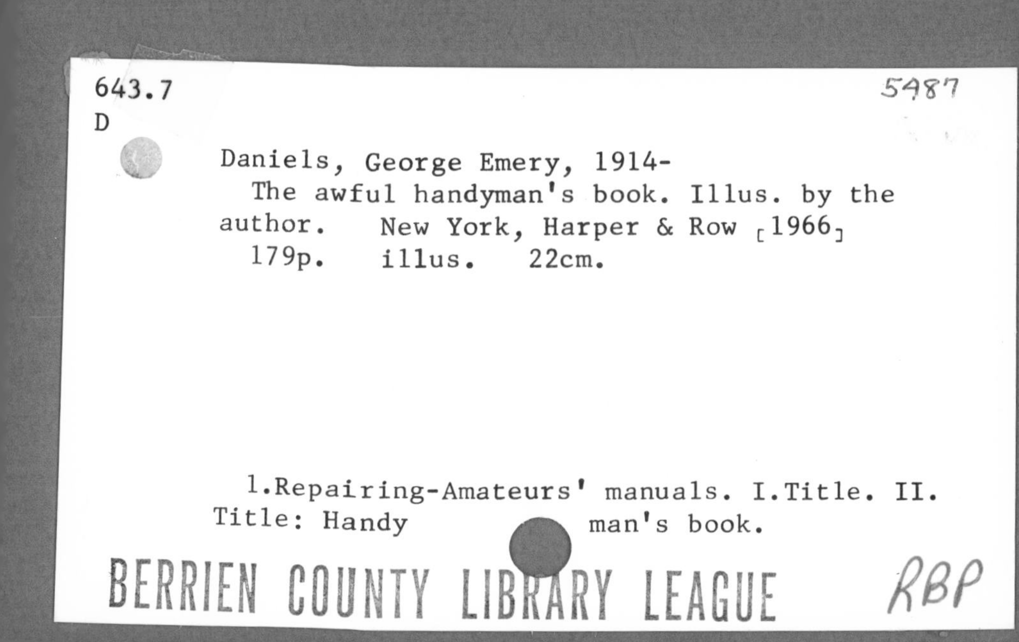

Daniels, George Emery, 1914-
The awful handyman's book. Illus. by the author. New York, Harper & Row [1966]
179p. illus. 22cm.

1.Repairing-Amateurs' manuals. I.Title. II. Title: Handy man's book.

THE AWFUL HANDYMAN'S BOOK

Books by George Daniels

THE AWFUL HANDYMAN'S BOOK

HOW TO BE YOUR OWN HOME ELECTRICIAN

HOW TO USE HAND AND POWER TOOLS

BUILD YOUR OWN MONSTROSITIES WITH TOOTH AND NAIL

THE PRACTICAL HOME HANDYMAN

HOW TO BUILD OR REMODEL YOUR HOME

THE EASY WAY TO MAKE AND REMODEL YOUR OWN FURNITURE

THE AWFUL HANDYMAN'S BOOK

by George Daniels

Illustrated by the author

HARPER & ROW, Publishers
New York, Evanston, and London

FIRST EDITION

LIBRARY OF CONGRESS CATALOG CARD NUMBER: 66-20732

CONTENTS

1

IT ONLY TAKES NERVE

THIS BOOK is for the millions (of both sexes) who fix things because they have to—whether they know how or not. It's for the dog-tired breadwinner who flops into his easy chair with the evening paper after a day's work, and finds the reading lamp won't work. It's for the harried housewife rushing from dishes to diapers to dinnertime—at which point the sink clogs up and overflows. It's for people who haven't the time to wait for help, or who don't enjoy paying for something they can do for nothing. It's definitely not for the tool-crazy fusspot who goes around squinting and snickering at other folks' hard-done handiwork. (For him a slap.) And it's not for master craftsmen or mechanical engineers, although they might come across something handy in it. (You get ideas from odd sources, sometimes.) Plainly, we're just offering ways of getting jobs done with a minimum of time, effort, skill, tools, and money. Even if you've never so much as driven a tack in your life, you can learn the tricks of the fix-it game in the pages that follow. But the chances are you'll never get around to driving that tack. There's usually a better way.

At the outset it's important to realize that your biggest problem isn't lack of know-how. It's lack of nerve. When you tackle something for the first time, it's likely to be a little scary, no matter what it is. And if you try it and make a botch of it, you'll probably end up disgusted. So get that first time over with in a way that can't scare you and can't turn out to be a flop. Before tackling a carpentry job, buy a 4-foot piece of 2 x 4 at the lumberyard, and some nails and screws. Then use the whole works to try out the tools you happen to own. (If you buy half a pound each of 2-inch common and 2-inch finishing nails, along with a dozen 1½-inch number 10 flathead steel screws, the left-overs are sure to come in handy later on. Let Chapter 2 be your guide as you use up the wood. Saw it, bore holes in it, plane it, drive nails in it and pull them out, drive screws. Give it the works. Even if your only tool is a hammer, drive a few nails. The knack comes quickly and does wonders for your confidence. You're not fixing anything or building anything so mistakes don't count. This is a practice session, pure and simple.

Apply the same general approach to other aspects of handy-manning, like the electrical repairs so many of us are squeamish about. Next time you're in the dime store, be bold and buy a lamp socket like the ones in the lamps around the house. Take it apart, put it together, and then keep it where you can find it. After you've seen it inside out, you won't be afraid to use it when one of those household lamps needs a replacement socket. Chapter 4 tells you exactly how to do it all in a matter of minutes. It's easy because electrical manufacturers have spent millions making it that way.

It's not sensible trying to rig up a practice fling at plumbing repairs. But, in the normal course of events, you won't have to wait too long before an opportunity to test your mettle in this field comes along naturally.

If there's anybody around who has the habit of telling you not to try any of these things because you'll probably bungle the job, banish that person from your working area. Unless you have a great sack of gold in the cellar, you have no choice but to become your own handyman. If you take it easy, you definitely won't bungle the job. And when you succeed, always remember to crow about it, and insofar as your detractors are concerned—rub it in.

Once you've actually done something downright useful with tools, even something like driving a picture hook into the wall and getting it in the right place (Chapter 10 explains it), you may decide that household fix-it, hang-it, and make-it jobs are really a pleasant form of diversion. Thousands of people think so. Although it's easier, it's a lot like golf. At first, when you're a duffer with the worst score on the course, you don't figure it's any fun at all. But after you've racked up a decent game or two, you may become an outright nut on the subject. As a home handyman, you may get that way, too. And, in a way, you have a much better game than golf. You always win, and you don't have to tip the caddy.

2

TOOLS YOU NEED AND HOW TO USE THEM

YOU CAN GET STARTED with just a handful of very simple tools, some of which you probably have already. A pocketknife, for example, is one you'll always need for hundreds of odd jobs, from scraping off dribbles of hardened paint to stripping insulation from the ends of lamp cord wires. If it's a Boy Scout knife, it even contains a screwdriver and a leather punch. The leather punch can also make a hole in soft wood—the kind of hole you might want to make in a wooden yardstick so it could be hung up on a nail. The kitchen ice pick is handy, too, for making much smaller holes in wood to get a screw started—as when you want to screw in some extra cup hooks. So much for the tools you may have right now.

SELECTING A HAMMER FOR YOUR NEEDS

A hammer should be one of the first tools you buy. You want a curved-claw nail hammer—the kind you see just about everywhere. The business end of the hammer head drives the nails, and the claws pull them out if you bungle the job, or if you're taking something apart. The curve of the claws lets you rock the handle backward in nail-pulling with minimum damage to the wood surface. That's why you don't want a straight-claw ripping hammer. That type is designed for jobs like ripping crates apart (although it can also drive nails). The straight claws are easier to jam between boards for prying, but they make a mess of the wood surface in nail-pulling because the other end of the head digs in as the hammer rocks back.

Your kind of hammer is size-rated according to the weight of its head, from around 7 ounces to 28 ounces. For everyday work, most men like a 16-ouncer, most women either a 12- or 14-ouncer. The even smaller lightweights are for delicate jobs like tacking, very fine cabinetwork, and modelmaking.

Many pros still prefer the feel of a wooden hammer handle, but it you're going to keep your hammer in a damp place like an unheated garage or in a hot place like a shelf next to the furnace,

The two major woodworking hammers. The roundly curved claw-type (right) is for general carpentry. It drives nails and also pulls them out—with minimum damage to the wood surface. The ripping hammer with relatively straight claws is suited to wrecking jobs, opening crates, and work where straight claws fit more easily between boards for prying apart.

you'll do better with a metal or fiberglass handle. These don't loosen from changes in humidity.

Before you buy any hammer, try swinging it a few times the way you would in driving a nail. If it has a comfortable, balanced feel in your hand, buy it. If not, try another type of handle. Generally, lighter-weight handles tend to feel more comfortable in action. And there can be quite a difference in weight between handles of hammers made by different manufacturers.

As to quality, you'll be using your hammer on many, many jobs, and for years to come—especially if you plan to build things. So pick one with a reputable name on it. The difference in price between the best and the worst is surprisingly small.

HOW TO DRIVE AND PULL NAILS

To drive a nail hold the nail, point on the wood, with the thumb and index finger of your left hand. Hold the hammer close to the end of the handle, *not* up near the head, with your right hand. (All this assuming you're right-handed.) Start the nail into the wood with several *light* hammer taps. *Don't slam it.* If you miss, you'll bang your fingers. At this stage you just want to get the nail far enough into the wood so it will stand up by itself. After that you can take your fingers out of the way and hit it harder. If you keep your eye on the nail, you'll be surprised at how good your aim is. Maybe it's instinctive. A hammer is a lot like a club, and people have been using clubs for a long time. And judging by some of the cracked skulls dredged up from the Stone Age, our ancestors had pretty good aim even then. If the nail starts to lean one way or the other in the early stages, tap it lightly to straighten it up. Pros do this while they're hammering by "drawing" the hammer stroke. If the nail is leaning outward, for example, they pull the hammer slightly inward as it hits the nail. You have to get the knack of this, however, so use the separate straightening-up taps until you've had more practice.

Most nail hammers are bell-faced, which means the striking surface of the head is slightly convex. Thus, if you drive the nail head down flush with the wood, the hammer makes only a slight hollow in the wood around the nail—not a dig. But if you're driving a finishing nail into something that's supposed to look nice, it's best to stop hammering when the nail head is just slightly above the surface. Then drive it slightly below the surface by resting a nail set on the nail head, and hitting the nail set. This little hammering accessory is simply a metal rod about the size of a half-length pencil. Like a pencil, it's pointed on one end, but the point is blunt so it can rest on the nail head. You can buy one wherever you buy your other tools.

Pulling a nail is easy if its head is still above the wood surface. If the head is flush with the surface or sunk below it, there are several ways to get it up enough to slip the hammer claws under it. If you can tap the nailed joint apart slightly and then tap it back together without hitting the nail, a common nail (the kind with a flat head) will usually be raised enough to let the pulling claws under it to finish the job. A finishing nail (the kind with a very small rounded head) is likely to sink even deeper when the joint is tapped open, however. So, if possible, tap the joint all the way open, forcing the nail head all the way through. Then pull the nail out of the other part of the joint with a pliers. When the joint can't be tapped open, it's usually a messy job to get the nail head up enough for pulling. You can blunt the point of a common nail by filing it; then rest it on top of a finishing nail head and

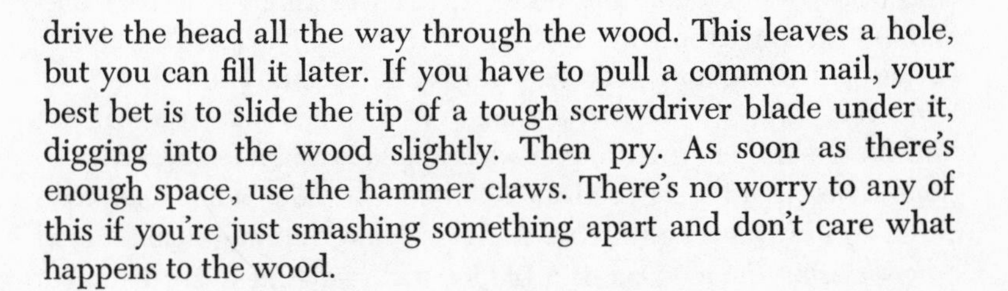

The nail set and center punch look alike except that nail set (right) has flat, blunt tip, the center punch a pointed tip.

drive the head all the way through the wood. This leaves a hole, but you can fill it later. If you have to pull a common nail, your best bet is to slide the tip of a tough screwdriver blade under it, digging into the wood slightly. Then pry. As soon as there's enough space, use the hammer claws. There's no worry to any of this if you're just smashing something apart and don't care what happens to the wood.

PLIERS FOR ALL-AROUND USE

Pliers should also be among your first tool buys. The kind you want at this stage are plain mechanic's pliers. They're also called slip-joint pliers because they have a two-position pivot that's not very conspicuous, but very handy. When it's in one position, you can close the jaws all the way to grip very small things, but you can't open them wide enough to grab the biggest things the pliers can handle. For the big things, you slip the pivot to the other position. Then the jaws can open wide. But they won't close all the way. Just shift them to suit the job.

According to the purists, just about everything we all do with these pliers is wrong, but don't worry about it. It's a horrible misuse, for example, to tighten a nut or bolt with them. You should use a wrench. But you'd need a binful of wrenches of all sizes and types to reach into the crannies and grab all the sizes you can with pliers. So if you occasionally chew the corner off a nut when your pliers slip, forget it. Nuts are cheap. Just relax in the knowledge that it's the useful misuses of pliers that make them so popular.

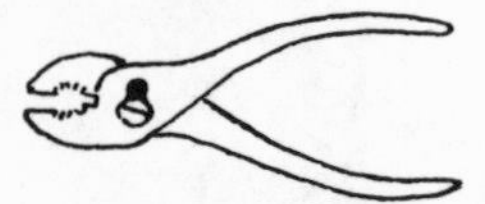

Slip-joint pliers, handiest type for general use. This pair has a notch type wire cutter.

Most slip-joint pliers will also cut wire, so buy the type that does. One form has a squared-off section near the back of each jaw for wire cutting. With the wire resting on one of these, you close the jaws to make the other squared section shear past the first one and cut the wire. This works if the pliers aren't wobbly at the joint, but they may get wobbly later on. Then they just bend the wire. To avoid the chance of this, you can buy pliers that have sharpened cutting blades in place of the squared sections. These blades seat tightly against each other when the jaws close, and bite through the wire. Even when the pliers have been banged around for years, the blades still cut almost all the way through the wire. So you need only give it a bend or two to break it off. But don't cut piano wire with pliers unless you are *sure* they're hardened for the purpose. If they're not, you'll just notch the cutting blades.

TYPES OF SCREWDRIVERS AND THEIR USES

While screwdrivers are probably made in a million shapes, sizes, and special forms, you can get along nicely with two or three, and add a funny one only when you need it. If you buy one with a blade tip width of 1/4 inch and another with a width of 5/16 inch, you can handle screws from size 6 to size 12—the most widely used sizes. This covers the standard screws with plain old slots across their heads. You'll also need at least one Phillips type screwdriver to fit the newer screws with the little crisscross hole in the head instead of a slot. A number 2 tip Phillips screwdriver will fit the screws you're most likely to encounter, as each tip size fits several screw sizes. If you ever want a set to fit all the sizes, all

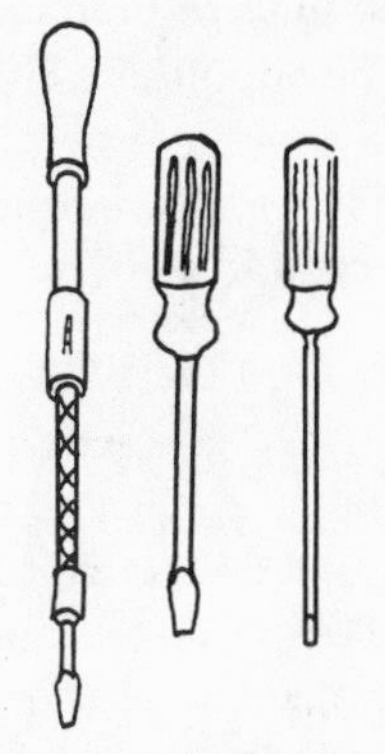

Handy screwdrivers. Start with simple ones. The conventional type (center) has a blade wider than its shaft. The cabinet, or electrician's, type (right) has a blade the same width as shaft. The Yankee type has crisscross spiral grooves on its shank. Push down on handle and it spins the screwdriver blade. You can set it with slide button to either drive or remove screws.

you need is four screwdrivers, as Phillips tips are numbered from 1 to 4. A handy length for all your screwdrivers is around 7 or 8 inches. Later on, for special jobs, you may want some longies, shorties, offsets, and what not. The offset screwdrivers have handles bent to right angles with the blade to give you leverage for turning hard-to-budge screws. You can also get a spiral ratchet screwdriver like the Yankee type that spins the screw two-and-a-half times when you push down on the handle. And these are just the beginning. It's a good idea somewhere along the line to buy a screwdriver with a cabinet blade (also called an electrician's blade). This is a long, skinny type with the flat tip of the blade only as wide as the round part of the shaft. Regular screwdriver blades are wider at the middle of the flat part. The skinny ones are great for reaching into holes to turn screws. You have to do this in lots of furniture and gadget repairs. One more handy form is the screw-holding screwdriver. This has little spring fingers at the end that hold the screw on the end of the blade so you can start it in a place too small for your fingers. There's also a split-blade type that does the same thing. Either one enables you to do certain ticklish jobs you couldn't do any other way.

AWLS, DRILLS, AND BIT BRACES

Hand tools for making holes take quite a few forms according to the kind of hole you want and what you want to make the hole in. The simplest is the awl. In the form of a scratch awl it's really just a short ice pick, and it also serves nicely as an ice pick. Just stick it into something, and you make a hole. Drag it along a surface, and you make a scratch—one way of marking for cutting,

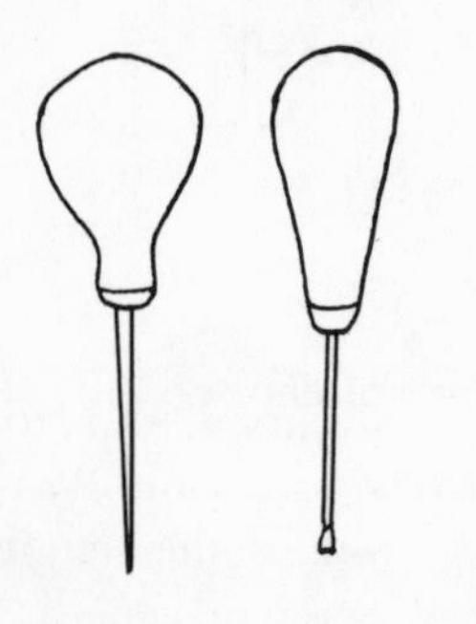

The two common awls—for hole making. The scratch awl (left) has a sharp point like an ice pick and can be used as one. It can be used for scratch-marking of wood or metal, and for making shallow holes. The brad awl (right) has a flattened tip that resembles a tiny screwdriver. By turning it back and forth, you can make larger and deeper holes without splitting than with the scratch awl. You can also use it as a fine-work screwdriver.

and so forth. You use this mainly to make little shallow holes in wood to start small screws. Just put the point of the screw in the hole, turn it with a screwdriver, and it pulls itself in the rest of the way. But don't try shoving the scratch awl deep into the wood or you may split the wood. The brad awl has a tiny flattened end on it like a miniature screwdriver. You turn it back and forth as you push it into the wood, so it cuts the wood fibers as it penetrates, instead of just wedging them apart like the scratch awl. Hence it can make a deep hole without splitting the wood. If you see one of these, buy it, for they're not as easy to find as scratch awls, but much handier. Many hardware stores don't stock them because they cost a little more than the others, and most people don't seem to know what's good about them. You can also use them as tiny screwdrivers, just in case you want to take your watch apart.

The hand drill is the standard hand tool for making holes up to ¼ inch diameter in wood, metal, or plastic. It has a big gear with a crank on one side of the handle, and one or two little gears on the handle itself. The lower of the little gears spins the chuck into

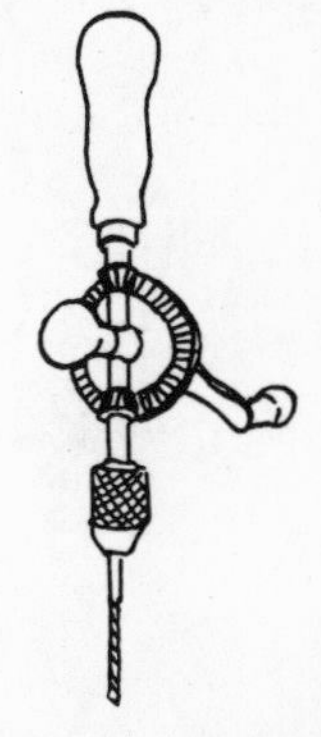

The hand drill is a long-popular tool for making small holes in wood, metal, and plastic. This one has small gears at the top and bottom of the large gear, increasing tool life.

which the drill bit fits. There are several kinds of chucks, but they all do the same thing. Turn the outer shell in one direction, and little jaws in the bottom of it open up. Push whatever size drill bit you want into the jaws and turn the shell the other way to tighten the bit in place. You use twist-drill bits in the hand drill. These have spiral fluting on them like the stripes on a candy cane. For most work you use carbon drills, which are much cheaper than high-speed drills. Either type will drill through anything from wood to metal, and the hole can be as deep as the drill bit is long.

To drill a hole in wood first punch a shallow hole in the surface with a nail or awl where you want the hole. In metal or plastic, use a center punch to make a little dent for a starter, so the drill bit won't skid across the surface. To do the drilling, apply moderate pressure to the top of the hand drill's vertical handle with your left hand while turning the crank with your right hand. Hold the tool steady, and don't let it tilt to and fro or you may break the drill bit. This is a lot easier if you apply muscle power to the crank only on the up-and-down portions of the cranking. All this is more important with very small-diameter bits than with

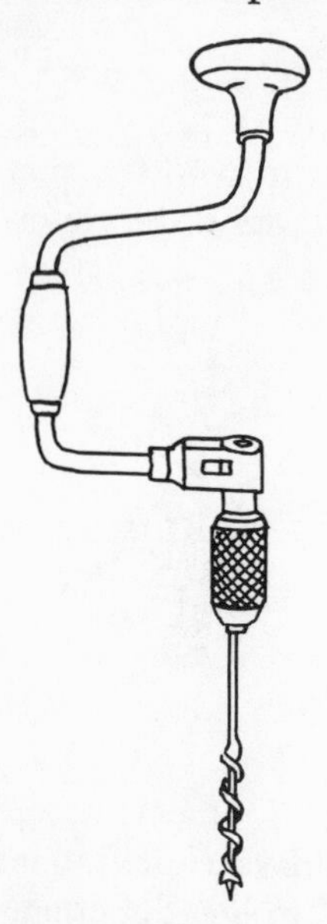

Bit brace with conventional auger bit. This is a crank-type tool for boring large holes in wood, smaller ones in metal. With countersink bit or screwdriver bit, it can also make recesses for flathead screw heads and drive the screws in.

fat ones. And the small ones are really small—some not much bigger around than a toothbrush bristle.

If you expect to drill lots of holes, it pays to buy a good hand drill. The ones with a little gear at both the top and bottom of the big gear are better than those with a little gear at the bottom only. The two gears keep the big one from developing wobble. Also, it's worthwhile to buy a model with a hollow, screw-capped vertical handle in which you can keep the assorted drill bits. Then you have them where you want them, and you won't lose them.

The push drill looks something like a fat screwdriver, and spins the drill bit when you push down on the handle. It's a good quick-job tool for making holes in wood and plastic, but its maximum hole diameter is usually only about ⅛ inch. It's handiest when the job calls for a lot of small holes of the same diameter, as in preparation for driving a big batch of screws.

The bit brace is the thing that looks like a shiny metal crank with a polished wooden knob on top. You see them hanging in most hardware stores. Its chuck takes either twist-drill bits (with special ends at the top) or auger bits that look like overgrown corkscrews. These come in sizes up to an inch in most brands, up to an inch and a half in a few. And you can buy an adjustable expansive bit (which is also fairly expensive) to make even bigger holes. The bit brace is used mainly for woodworking, though its twist-drill bits will also drill metal. One handy bit for it

Countersink bit like this fits the bit brace to make conical recesses for flathead screw heads.

is the countersink bit, which makes the shallow conical recesses at the top of holes drilled for screws. This lets the heads of flathead screws sink in flush with the wood surface.

If you're going to drill something hard like metal or plastic, make a dent in it first with a center punch where you want the hole. (Don't use an auger bit except for wood.) Then set the point of the drill bit in the dent and crank the bit brace in a clockwise direction. Hold the top knob in your left hand and bear down on it slightly while turning the crank with your right. Do everything the same way when boring wood, but you can skip the center punch, as the tip of the auger bit has a sharp point to make its own starting hole. You can also buy a pipe-reamer bit for this tool and misuse it in many wonderful ways. It looks like a big, conical, straight-fluted arrowhead, and it's supposed to be used to take the sharp burrs from the inside of cut pipe. But it's great for enlarging holes in wood or metal when you don't happen to have the right size bit in the first place.

A good bit brace doesn't cost much more than a poor one so you might as well treat yourself to the best. You could spend more for a quart of gin.

SAWS AND SAWING

There are all kinds of saws, but the one you're most likely to use a lot is the crosscut saw. This, as you may have guessed, is designed to cut *across* the grain of the wood, as in cutting the end off a board. (A ripsaw cuts lengthwise—which you're not likely to do often.) The teeth of the crosscut saw are shaped like little daggers, while those of a ripsaw are like little chisels, so be sure you get a crosscut for crosscutting. The difference in teeth makes a big difference. There's also some choice in the number of teeth per inch (called points), but this is of interest mainly to fussy people. In general, finer teeth make a smoother-surfaced cut but don't cut as fast. Coarse teeth cut faster and make a slightly rougher cut. Your best bet: get a good quality saw and don't count teeth. Don't buy a cut-rate saw. With a good one you can actually cut through 1-inch white pine at close to 10 feet per minute with ease. With a cheap saw you can wear yourself out going less than half as fast.

If you're likely to be cutting any damp, green, or pitchy wood, look for a saw with a taper-ground blade. This is actually thinner at the back edge (away from the toothed edge) than at the toothed edge. And it's thinner at the narrow tip than at the handle end. As a result, it breezes through sticky wood that would jam an ordinary saw so you might even have a tough time pulling it out. As the hardware clerk may not know what you're talking about when you ask for one (even though he has them in stock), it may be best to ask for it by name and number. The Disston D-23 crosscut saw is a good example. This one has a straight-backed edge to the blade, like a ruler. And you can use it to draw straight lines for cutting. Many craftsmen, however, prefer skew-backed saw blades (which are also available taper-ground), but you can't use them for drawing straight lines as the edge has a long curve. Otherwise one works as well as the other, and even the saw manufacturers don't know why such a bunch of people like the curved ones. So don't let blade shape bother you.

How to saw

To start the cut, make a few draw strokes with the butt end of the blade (near the handle) to make a notch for the blade. Then go ahead with full strokes—easy, not fast. With too much speed the blade can jump out of its cut and dig up the wood somewhere else before you can stop it. Or it can dig into the hand with which you're holding the wood. Just let the weight of the saw ride easy and do the work. It's a cinch.

If you've marked something to exact length, make your cut on the waste side of the pencil line—so the saw cut, itself, is in the throwaway piece. If you're aiming for a precision job where something has to fit snug, the width of the saw cut can make it loose. If you cut the thing just a shade too long, you can trim it off with coarse sandpaper on a block. But if you do happen to cut something too short, don't burst into tears. You can always fill in the gap with a sliver of wood and some glue. Another cheerful thing about sawing is the fact that you can actually steer the saw as you go along if you notice your cut is running cockeyed. Just flex the blade *very* slightly toward the direction you want it to go, and it will veer the cut in that direction.

The hacksaw comes in handy for a lot of unglamorous jobs like sawing through rusty bolts when the nuts won't unscrew, or cutting curtain rods to length. Although you're not likely to need one of these saws often, you're likely to need it plenty when you need it at all. So it's handy to have around. You use fine teeth for thin material, coarse teeth for thick stuff. About 14 teeth per inch is right for soft steel, iron, brass, bronze, copper, and aluminum. Use 18 teeth per inch for iron pipe and angle iron that you might cut for a railing or part of junior's home-grown pushmobile. For hard stuff, 24 teeth per inch generally works best. And for very thin sheet metal, 32 teeth per inch gets the nod. Mount the blade in the hacksaw frame so the teeth are leaning forward like the teeth on your crosscut saw.

In using the hacksaw, first be sure whatever you're going to cut is held firmly so it can't shift while you're sawing. If it shifts, it can break the blade. (Some kind of a vise is handy for the firm-holding job in most cases. You can buy little ones that clamp on a table if you don't have a workbench. If you have a workbench, get a vise that bolts on with a swiveling base that lets you turn it around to any position you want.) Hold the saw with the handle in your right hand, and grip the upper front corner of the frame with your left hand. Bear down moderately on the forward stroke and ease off the pressure on the back stroke. That's all there is to it.

TIPS ON USING AND SHARPENING PLANES

Planes save the day when you have to shave a little wood off the edge of a sticky door.

The handiest plane for your starting kit is a block plane. This is a little one you can hold in one hand while holding the work with the other. When you buy it, get the kind that has a little knurled knob on a screw shaft that runs parallel to the angle of the blade. All this is pretty much out in the open where you can see it. If you're not sure it's the right kind, try turning the little knob at the back. Turning it clockwise should make the blade stick out farther through the bottom of the plane. Turning it the other way should pull the blade back in again. It'll take a couple of turns each way to see what it does. If it does what it's supposed to do, that's it. There's a cheaper kind that has a flat, lump-edged little wheel lying right on top of the rear end of the blade. With this type you turn the wheel counterclockwise to loosen the blade. Then you push the blade to stick out through the bottom as far as you want it, after which you turn the wheel the other way to tighten things up. This is a nuisance for the beginner, and not much handier for the pro. So spend a little more and get the easy one.

If you've never used a plane before, try it out on a piece of practice wood before you tackle something important. This will show you how the thing works and how to adjust it. After that it's a breeze.

First, take a look at the bottom of the plane, and turn the adjusting knob. You'll notice that as the blade sticks farther out of the slot in the bottom, it also narrows the open space in the slot. As this is the space the shaving must pass through, the blade should always be adjusted so there's plenty of open space for the shaving—which means the blade shouldn't stick out very far. (If it does, it digs into the wood too much, anyway.) In general, the shaving shouldn't be thicker than a calling card. For final smoothing, it should be more like paper. You don't try to take off a ton of wood with a plane. If a wide strip has to come off, you can saw it off, then plane it smooth. Figure on the plane when less than ¼ inch has to be taken off. (You can shave off a lot more, but you'll

The plane at the left is going in correct direction to make smooth shavecut. The plane at right will chip wood surface, make rough cut. Always look at grain on side of wood being planed, and plane uphill. If you can't see grain, but the plane makes a rough cut, try planing in opposite direction.

get fed up with planing.) You can also use the plane to bevel or round the edge of a board. Just tip it as you work.

Always plane in the uphill direction of the grain, as shown in the drawing. This leaves a smooth surface. If you plane in the downhill direction of the grain, the blade hooks into the grain ends and leaves a rough, chipped-out surface.

To keep the blade sharp, remove it from the plane (it's easy to do, as the hardware dealer can show you) and dress the edge on a flat oilstone. You can buy the stone where you buy the plane. The easy way: hold the bevel of the cutting edge flat on the stone—so the length of the blade sticks up from the stone at the corresponding angle. Then slide the blade back and forth a few times. For the final touch, tip the blade to a slightly steeper angle and repeat the process. This sharpens the very edge. Put some thin oil on the stone (like number 10 engine oil) to keep fine metal particles from clogging it. Finish the job by laying the blade flat on the stone with the beveled side of the cutting edge up, and sliding it back and forth a couple of times. This smooths off the tiny bent-over edge formed by stoning the bevel. All this is easier with a little gadget called a plane iron sharpener. You just clamp the plane blade (technically called the plane iron) in the thing and move it back and forth over the stone. Millers Falls Company (tools) makes one. Either way, you'll get the sharpening knack quickly.

HANDY SMALL POWER TOOLS

Power tools are now so numerous and varied that you can fill a cellar with them and still be lacking some basic types. About the best one to start off with is the power drill. A little ¼-inch one

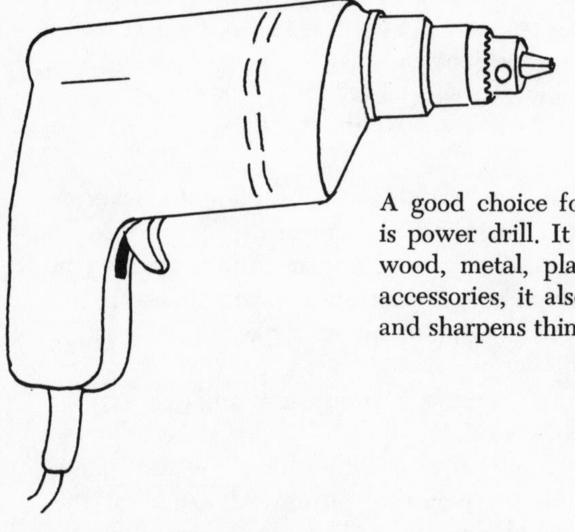

A good choice for your first power tool is power drill. It makes holes quickly in wood, metal, plastic, or masonry. With accessories, it also sands, polishes, saws, and sharpens things.

should do the trick. (The sizes are based on the maximum-diameter drill bit that will fit in the chuck.) It can, of course, bore holes in almost anything (even concrete with a masonry bit) much faster than a hand drill. But that's the least of its wonders. With a flexible sanding disk, it can sand off old paint at a furious rate, or chew away wood so fast you can actually shape things with it. And if you want to do a smooth sanding job, as in preparing for a fine natural wood finish, you can use a rigid ball-jointed sanding disk like the Stanley Swirlaway. Both types have shafts that fit the chuck, and they take all the usual abrasive grades from coarse to fine.

The power drills themselves vary widely in price, and almost every tool manufacturer makes them. Unless you're opening a factory, you'll do fine with the economy model rather than the heavy-duty type. And you'll do better with an American make than an import in case you need a replacement part sometime. Watch the newspapers for sales of power tools, and shop around. Also hint like crazy. You might get one for your birthday. You'll usually save money if you buy just the power drill and whatever specific attachment (like a sanding disk) you actually need. If you bite for the Grand De Luxe Super All-Purpose Kit, you may pay as much as you would for a couple of power drills and end up with a string of gadgets you don't need—plus a handsome metal carrying case and no place to put it. Although prices are forever shifting, power drills and men's shoes usually seem to be in the same range, grade for grade.

How to drill with a power drill

Follow the same starting procedures as with a hand drill. Then put the drill bit on the spot where you want the hole, pull the trigger, and push a little. In wood the thing works so fast it's all over in a second. In metal it's fast, too. So it's wise to put a drop of oil in the hole after you've drilled a little, to lubricate the bit. This is where a high-speed bit may be worthwhile, too.

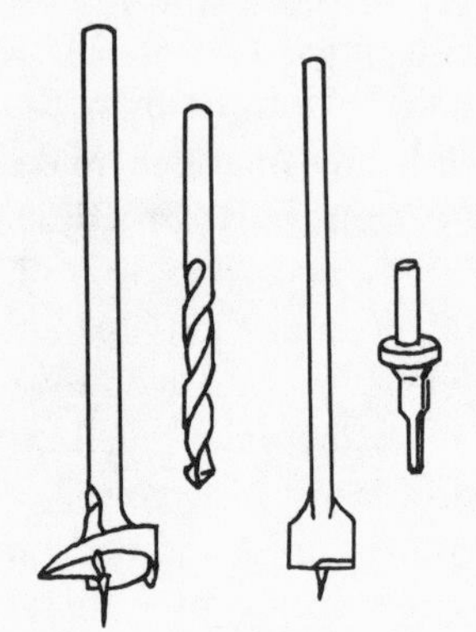

Left to right: The Stanley Power-Bore bit. This type is smooth-boring and well suited to cabinet and precision work. The twist drill bit is fluted in candy-stripe fashion. It can make holes in wood, plastic, or metal. For slow-turning hand drills you can use the carbon-type twist drill which is in the lowest price range. For fast work with a power drill ask for high-speed bits which cost a little more but last longer at higher revolutions per minute. The flat-ended spade bit does the same kind of work as the Power-Bore but may vibrate a little more and lack some of the smoothness of the other type. But it's lower priced. The multibore bit (like the screwmate) drills the correct wood screw diameters for the counter-sunk head, smooth screw shank, and screw thread in a single operation. A slightly different form also drills the hole for a wooden plug to cover the screw head. Just ask for the form you want. Tip: in boring through wood watch for the pointed tip of the bit. When it pokes through the far side of the wood, pull the bit out, re-insert it in the other surface of the wood (where the tip poked through) and finish boring from that side. This avoids splitting out the surface as the bit emerges.

How to sand with a power drill

With a flexible sanding disk, tip the drill so the disk flexes against the work, with about half of the disk area (the outer half) in contact. The motion at the contact area should be generally in the direction of the grain. And *keep the disk moving along the work.* If you hold it in one spot for even a few seconds, it will cut a deep gouge that's very tough to sand away. Just keep at the job until you get the result you want. With a ball-jointed Swirlaway simply rest the disk flat on the surface of the work and keep it moving along.

What a saber saw is and how to use it

The saber saw is one of the real humdingers of the portable power-tool field. Its granddaddy was an American signmaker's tool called the Cutawl, which has been in use for half a century. Yet the first actual saber saw to hit the American market came from Switzerland's Scintilla Company around twenty years ago. Now almost everybody makes them. And for good reason. They can cut wood, metal, or plastic along straight lines, curves, or bevels, and even make their own starting holes in the mid-area of a panel—as when you want to cut a window in a flush door. And

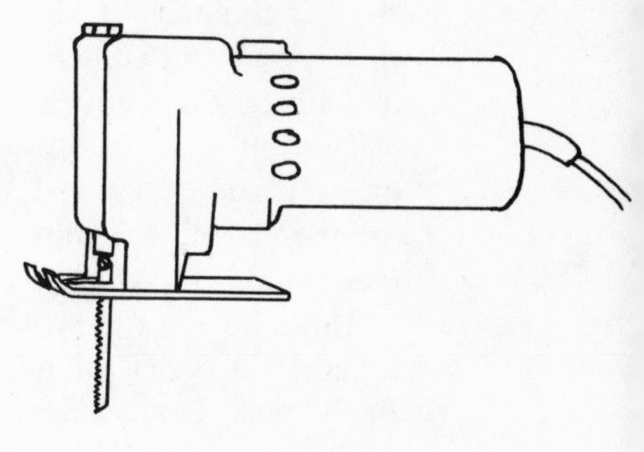

The saber saw is the most versatile portable power saw. It cuts wood, metal, or plastic (with blades for each purpose) along straight or curved lines. It's also one of the safest of power saws.

they're just about the safest power saws ever devised. Husbands like them because they make it easy to build anything from a workbench to a cabin cruiser. And wives like them because they can cut a frozen steak in half, including the bones, without thawing. Also they look and handle a lot like a portable kitchen mixer.

Essentially, the saber saw consists of a metal body with a little motor or vibrator in it, and a flat base underneath with about a 3- or 4-inch straight saw blade sticking downward through it.

When the saw is turned on, the blade moves up and down several *thousand* times a minute.

To make a cut, first pencil-mark the line you want to cut. Then rest the flat base of the saw on the surface of the thing you'll be cutting, with the blade not quite touching the edge it is to cut into. Push the starting button (or pull the trigger, depending on the kind of switch the saw has), and move the blade gently into the wood. From there on, just push it easily and steer it along the line. It's so simple novices often can't quite believe it. If you're resting a board on a table to support it while cutting, just be sure you don't cut the table in half. It's easier than you think.

If you want to cut a hole in the middle of something, like that window in the door, you first pencil the outline of the opening. Then stand the saber saw on its nose with the tip of the blade resting on some part of the line to be cut. Then turn the thing on (but hang on to it), and *very slowly* tip it backward so the blade cuts into the wood. When the saw is resting flat on its base, just steer it the rest of the way along the line to finish the cut. As this tip-in stunt calls for a steady hand, don't tackle it until you've had a little plain cutting experience.

The tool gets its operating safety from the fact that very little of the blade is exposed above the work where your hands are. In order to touch the moving blade—don't ever do it—you'd have to reach under the work. So simply keep your hands on top.

Though prices vary, you can usually get a workshop model for around the price of a power drill. The Forsberg Company, of Bridgeport, Connecticut, makes a lightweight model in this category. If you plan on really heavy work, you can get a bigger one like Stanley's H-75. Your best bet: shop around and pick a reputable brand in the size you want.

MEASURING AND MARKING TOOLS

One of the handiest modern measuring tools is the flexible steel tape rule. You can buy one of these at any hardware store. Lengths range up to 10 feet, sometimes even more, yet the whole length of the flexible steel rule rolls up into a case not much bigger than a cigarette lighter. For average work, an 8-footer is about right. In the usual form, the tape slides out easily as you pull it, and rolls back into the case automatically when you let go of it. To make things as easy as possible for yourself, however, you'll do well to pick one of the types that have a brake. With these, you can push a button to make the measuring tape stay out when you want it to, without holding it. When you want it to roll up, you just give the button another push (or push it the other way) and the tape slithers back into its case. Both types are in the low price range as tools go.

To mark a right angle, the simplest tool is a "try" square. The name comes from the fact that it was originally used to try the cut-off end of something to see if it was square. This tool comes in several forms, basically similar. The usual type has a metal blade with the edges marked in inches, and a thicker handle forming an

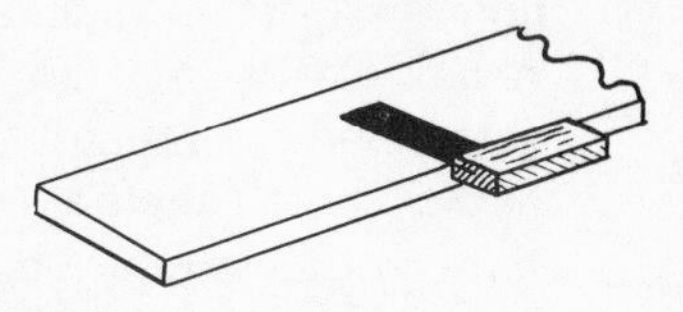

The "try" square is L-shaped with a thin blade and thick portion called the handle. Set the handle against the edge of a board and the blade extends across it at right angles to the edge. Draw your penciled cutting line along the blade.

L with the blade. If you want to mark a pencil line across a board at right angles so you can cut it off square, just set the handle firmly against the edge of the board and draw a pencil line along the edge of the blade. Then saw along the pencil line. A variation called a combination square also lets you mark 45-degree angles that you might want for corner joints, as the miters in picture frames. Ask to see one at your hardware store. It does all the things a try square can do and a lot more. Some models even include bubble tubes so they can serve as levels. And all of them have a removable blade that serves as a precision ruler. They cost more than try squares, but they serve more purposes. So look them over before you buy a try square.

Buy other tools as you need them

With the hand and power tools described in these pages, you can actually build a house or a cabin sloop and almost all kinds of furniture, except maybe a piano. In fact, this was written in a seven-room house built with fewer tools than have been mentioned. And the same tools built a cabin sloop and a batch of tables, chairs, and cabinets that have appeared in magazines from coast to coast. So it doesn't take a truckload of fancy tools to fix and make things. Basically, you need a little practice, a lot of nerve, and a few bucks for materials.

Now and then a job you tackle will call for some tool you don't happen to have. If it's something inexpensive or something you're likely to use all the time, it usually pays to buy it. Sooner or later you'll probably want two or three different-sized chisels, for example. If you want a big tool with a good-sized price tag, like a table saw, shop around for it. It's the kind of thing you'll probably get a lot of use out of if you plan to go hog-wild on building things. But if you want something like a big portable chain saw to cut up a dead tree that tumbles into your back yard, you may not need the tool again. So, since it's expensive, rent it. Tool-rental places like the United Rent-All Stores are all over the place, and the rental cost is only a small fraction of the purchase price. There's another advantage, too. The rental store owner will show you how to use the thing you rent, and he'll do it carefully. That way you learn something you didn't know before, and you don't bust up his tool.

3

PLUMBING—WHERE TROUBLE WON'T WAIT

A SCRATCH on your gleaming walnut Steinway may shake you to the core, but it doesn't call for instant action. A stopped-up sink, fed by the steady dribble of a leaky faucet and ready to overflow, is an altogether different matter, however. For plumbing troubles are the meanest, most demanding household nuisances you're likely to encounter. That's why they've been given first position in this book. If you've never faced this type of headache, you may not know it's likely to make its sneaky attack without warning—in the middle of the night when you're dead-tired and couldn't get a plumber even if you could afford one. So get ready. They can't lick you. But you may have a real fight on your hands. To get in trim we'll take the simplest troubles first.

HOW TO FIX THAT LEAKY FAUCET

The dripping faucet can turn up any time. But you'll probably notice it first in the wee, silent hours of the night as you toss to the infernal blip—blap—blip of the ailing bathroom faucet. You wring that faucet shut with all the strength in your hands; you shut every door that can seal it away from you. But still you hear it. You know it will never stop. You long to wrench the evil thing out by its very roots, but you know you can't. And it's just as well. There's a better way.

When you can't kill it, silence it!

Just douse a washcloth in water and wrap its upper end around that hellish faucet. Twist the rest of the cloth in a spiral drape downward to the bottom of the basin, tub, or sink. And let it rest to one side of the drain. The water won't drip any more. It will simply soak down the washcloth and trickle away silently into the night—through the plumbing. You haven't cured the trouble but you've muffled it, and you'll get your sleep. If the cloth shows a

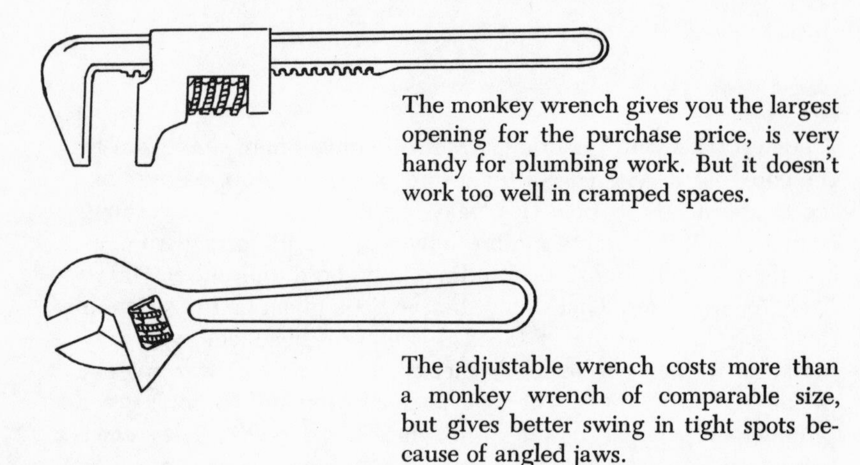

The monkey wrench gives you the largest opening for the purchase price, is very handy for plumbing work. But it doesn't work too well in cramped spaces.

The adjustable wrench costs more than a monkey wrench of comparable size, but gives better swing in tight spots because of angled jaws.

yearning to slip off the end of the faucet spout, put a rubber band or a tight loop of string around it. When you want to use the faucet, you need only flip the cloth up and back, out of the way. And at the end of the following day you can tear that faucet apart, rip out its vitals, and put it together again so it will drip no more—maybe for at least a year or so. More about this immediately.

Replace the washer for total victory

To replace the faucet washer that caused your troubles, you need a wrench big enough to grip the hexagonal cap on the faucet and screw it off. The plain old monkey wrench of yesteryear is top-notch for the job if your hardware dealer can find one at the back of some musty old drawer. (Heavy-duty ones are still made for plumbers.) Price for price, its jaws open wider than those of today's fancy wrenches. But it doesn't get as good a swing in close quarters. If you can't find one, however, pay a bit more and get a more modern form big enough to do the job.

If your plumbing is aristocratic, you'll find little valves in the pipes under your sinks just below both faucets. Then you can shut off the valve under the faucet you're about to repair, and leave everything else turned on. If these little valves are lacking, you'll have to shut off all the water temporarily while you make your repairs. The main water valve is usually in the cellar.

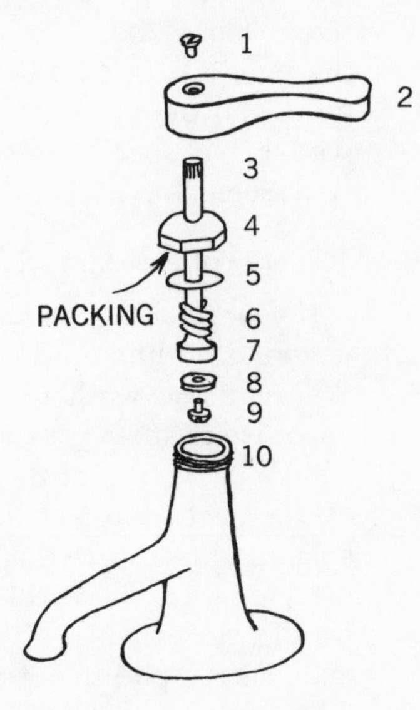

Faucet parts. This is what you find when you take faucet apart to replace a washer. The screw at the top (1) holds the handle (2) to the shaft (3). You can shift the handle position, then tighten the screw to hold it. Some types have a splined shaft (equally spaced grooves) as shown, others are square. The hexagonal cap (4) is the part you remove with the wrench from the faucet body. Anti-shaft leak packing is up inside it, as shown by arrow. The washer below it (5) holds the packing firm. Big screw threads (6) at the lower end of the shaft turn the faucet on and off. The small drum-shaped metal cup (7) at the base of the shaft holds the washer (8). The screw (9) shown below locks the washer in place. The faucet body is (10).

The first step is removing the hexagonal cap from the top of the faucet body. (The faucet shaft runs through the center of it.) Wrap a piece of bandaging adhesive tape, or something like it, around the hexagonal section before you grip it with the wrench. This protects the shiny chrome from scratches. Then turn it counterclockwise. To get it all the way off, you may have to give the faucet handle a turn or two in the "on" direction to raise the shaft. This may be to either left or right, depending on the faucet. Once the hex cap is free, keep turning the faucet handle in the "on" direction until you can lift the whole business out of the faucet body.

If you now take the part you've pulled out and turn it upside down, you'll see a fiber washer is held in the bottom of it by a screw through the center. This washer is the worn-out thing that has been causing the drip. Surprisingly, the screw usually comes out easily. But you may have to pry the edge of the washer with a penknife to lift it out. Match a new washer to it from your box assortment, and put the new one where the old one was, fastening it in with the same old screw. If your washer assortment includes a few new screws, as some do, you can replace the screw, too. Either way, once the washer is replaced, you can put the faucet back together. If, however, you're the devil-may-care type who doesn't read labels, you'd better check to see if the washer box specifies one color washer for hot water, another for cold. Some do.

The case of the skewed faucet handle

If your faucet has a single-arm handle, you'll probably find that it stops at a different point from its mate when it's shut off, after replacing the washer. This irksome lack of symmetry is easily remedied in most instances by removing the screw that holds the handle to the top of the faucet shaft, and tapping the handle up off the shaft. Most of the fancy-style faucets have their handles splined to the shaft. This means that little teeth protruding from the top of the shaft (like gear teeth) fit similar teeth inside the handle. So you can align the handle a tooth at a time until it matches the position of its mate on the other faucet, then tighten it back in place with the screw.

Faucets that dribble around their shafts

If, when turned on, your faucet dribbles a little cascade around the shaft, the trouble lies in the packing around the shaft, and it's easy to cure. In the usual case the packing is a mildly mushy fibrous stuff inside the hexagonal cap on the faucet body. A metal washer under it squashes it into a tapered recess inside the cap as the cap is tightened down, squeezing it against the shaft. But the packing sometimes stiffens up with time and refuses to squash. So your faucet gets the dribbles. To make things shipshape, buy a little package of graphite faucet packing at your hardware store. It's inexpensive, and in its handiest form it looks like a small coil of shiny black vermicelli. To use it, pull the metal washer down (after shutting off the water and removing the faucet cap) and wrap a single turn of the black vermicelli around the shaft, up against the old packing. You can push it into the space around the shaft with your fingernails or a very small screwdriver—just enough to hold it. When you tighten everything back together, the new packing gets squished into the leak space around the shaft and stops the dribble. If the dribble doesn't stop, add more packing.

WHEN A DRAIN IS CLOGGED

When a plumbing fixture overflows or refuses to drain, there are usually some plain clues that tell you whether you need a particular fix-it tool or a plumber. In general, if only one fixture, such as a washbasin, is affected, and everything else is working just fine, the trouble is easy to cure. If drainage from the basin backs up into the bathtub or into a fixture on the floor below, you *may* need a plumber. The more serious foul-ups, however, aren't very common, so let's tackle the easy ones first.

Instant cure—often possible

Begin with a quick check of the clogged fixture's outlet. A matting of hair, lint, and soap film tends to build gradually on accessible (but not readily visible) strainer and stopper mechanism parts in tub and basin outlets. This matting often seals up completely with surprising suddenness. Roll up your sleeve, reach down through the water, and pull out anything that feels like this kind of blockage. This often ends the trouble without further ado. You can complete the job with tweezers after the fixture empties.

Cleaning a trap

When the instant cure doesn't work, the next suspect on the list is the trap under the fixture. This is a shiny section of pipe with an obvious U-bend in it. It's designed to retain a pocket of water in the bottom of the U to act as a seal against sewer gas and bacteria that would otherwise escape into the house through the plumbing fixtures. But the trap also retains assorted items that tumble down the fixture outlet. Clogged kitchen sink traps often contain such things as missing butter knives, pickle forks, and other bits of flatware. And many a plumber, called in desperation, has made the headlines by retrieving diamond rings, pearl necklaces, and other posh trinkets from plumbing traps. To make his work and yours easier, most traps have a good sized screw-in plug at the bottom of the U. Before you put a wrench on the hexagonal head of the plug for the grand opening, however, scoop as much water as possible out of the fixture. Then place a bucket under the trap to catch the rest.

The glop, but not always the treasure, comes out of the drain-plug hole quickly. If there's no sign of stringy or matted material that might have caused clogging, use a flashlight to get a good look down the fixture outlet. If there's anything there but empty space, wiggle a piece of wire around inside the pipe. Solid objects from forks to jewelry can often be snared and lifted up through the outlet with a hook-ended wire. (This is much easier than dismantling the trap connections to do the job.) When everything is cleared, smear the threads on the drain plug with a little pipe joint compound (often called pipe dope) and screw it back in place, but not with brute strength. The joint compound (like sticky paint that never dries) seals the plug without excessive tightening, and makes it easier to remove the next time. (A small can costs very little and lasts for years of plumbing fix-it jobs.)

The force cup

When a drain pipe is clogged at some point beyond the trap, the wooden-handled rubber force cup (sometimes called a plumber's helper) is the first tool to try. If you plan to use it in a double sink, a washbasin with an overflow opening, or a bathtub with a similar overflow, you'll do well to persuade some willing soul to help you by holding a cellulose sponge against the overflow opening while you pump with the force cup. Otherwise you'll have to hold the sponge with one hand and pump with the other. If you don't block the overflow, you're likely to shower the entire room with your first good squish. In a double sink, your helper can simply hold the stopper tight in the second sink, in most cases. The reason for all this: as you force the water down the drain, it takes the easiest route–up the overflow pipe or the second drain of a double sink. Aside from showering the room, you waste the power that should be driving the stoppage out of the drain pipe.

To get the full effect of the force cup, try to catch the rhythm of the water surge in the pipe. There should be enough water in the fixture to cover most of the force cup. As you push it down, water will rise in the overflow, but it can't get out. As you release the cup, the water will drop in the overflow pipe. At a fairly slow but even tempo, you'll usually feel a slight assist in your pumping action from the natural reversal of the water. At intervals of around half a minute, lift the cup forcibly from the drain opening and watch to see if the water flows out. Don't worry about the grime that churns loose from the inside of the pipe and rises into the fixture. It's easy to wash it away when the pipe is cleared. As soon as the pipe clears and the water drains, follow it with a potful of very hot water to melt any greasy deposit that may have collected at the stoppage point. Trouble-saving tip: you can usually avoid stoppages entirely if you use your force cup as soon as you notice a slow-down in drainage from a fixture. Use the cup while water still remains in the fixture, closing the overflow, as usual, and applying a few energetic pumping strokes. As the pumped water flows *through* the narrowed opening in the pipe where a stoppage is building up, the higher speed of the flow does a rapid clearing job.

Using the snake

When a drain pipe is too solidly blocked for the force cup to free it, you need a drain and trap auger, more widely known as a plumber's snake. The body of the snake (usually 15 to 25 feet long) consists of a flexible wire backbone with a layer of smaller wire wrapped tightly around it from end to end. The end you push into the pipe usually has a twisted wire tip on it resembling an arrowhead. A hollow metal crank handle slides along the length of the snake. Tighten the setscrew of the crank at any point, and you can rotate whatever length of snake you have inside the pipe. For general use, be sure you buy a drain and trap auger (there are heavier types) as it is flexible enough to flex into the pipe from the drain opening in most traps.

To speed the job, slide the snake into the pipe a few inches at a time and give it a turn or two whenever it seems to meet tough going. If it appears to be really blocked, you may have reached the trouble spot. At this point combine the turning with a back-and-forth movement of an inch or so, working it ahead gradually until it feels free again. In most modern houses the entire run of

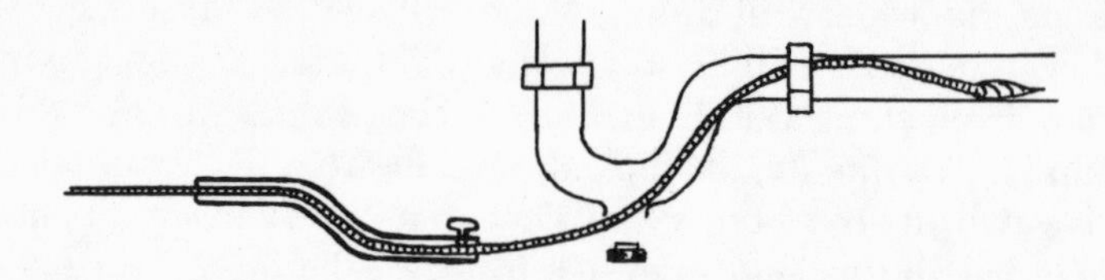

How a plumber's snake slips through a drain pipe. If the trap has no clean-out plug, remove large hexagonal nuts at each end of the trap section (where it joins other pipe) and remove the trap completely. This requires a little gentle wiggling of trap, freeing one end, then the other. After this simply push the snake into the drain pipe.

drain pipe from any fixture to the sewer stack (the large diameter vertical pipe) is much less than the snake's length. You can tell where the stack is by looking at your roof. You'll see a large open-ended vent pipe protruding through the roof somewhere above the bathroom area. That's the top of the stack. It's open to prevent sewer gas from building up in the plumbing, and to let air in for a free outflow of waste water. Once you know where the stack is, don't waste time and effort pushing more snake into the drain pipe than necessary to reach the stack. That's where the job ends.

Pulling the snake out after clearing the pipe is a bit more pleasant if you grasp the grimy thing with old rags, and wipe it as you go. Then hose it off before you coil it up for storing. If you think you'll never be the same after such a messy episode, console yourself. Plumbers do it every day.

WHEN TO CALL THE PLUMBER

If your bathroom washbasin's contents flow out freely and end up in the bathtub, you have learned something about your plumbing layout. You know that both basin and tub are on the same drain leading to the stack. And you know something is clogged. If the bathroom is on the second floor and nothing is backing up into fixtures on the first floor, the trouble is very likely in the drain pipe from tub to stack. And the chances are you can fix it by one of the methods just described. The bathtub trap, however, may be located some distance from the tub, as a trap directly under a tub is hardly in a convenient spot. If you can't find the bathtub trap and can't clear the stoppage with either force cup or snake, call a plumber. And watch what he does. If it's not too much work, you may decide to do it yourself if it's ever necessary again. The reason for skipping the job yourself: in some instances, fortunately rare, work may be required inside a wall or under a floor. An experienced plumber can do it with less fuss than you can—and probably save you money, at that.

If, heaven forbid, all the fixtures, including the toilet, back up into the bathtub or into the fixtures on the floor below, it's likely that your house sewer (the main outgoing pipe line) is clogged. Fixing this is not a fitting task for the fastidious homeowner, so put your tools away and call the plumber. He will do the trick by removing a big screw-in clean-out plug from the sewer line in your basement, and inserting a sewer rod, perhaps a power-driven cleaning auger. If you *must* do this job yourself, you'll do well to rent the tools—for two reasons. First, the tool rental agent can give you some good firsthand instruction on using the tools. And, second, if a power-driven auger is needed to clean the sewer line (as when tree roots have worked their way into it), the purchase price of the tool is far higher than the cost of a professional plumbing job. But the rental cost is low enough to make it practical.

HOW A FLUSH TANK WORKS

Commonest of the toilet troubles is the singing toilet. You can usually stop the singing by merely jiggling the handle on the flush tank. But if that doesn't do the job, a little handy-man activity is required. This is much easier when you know how the flush tank's innards work.

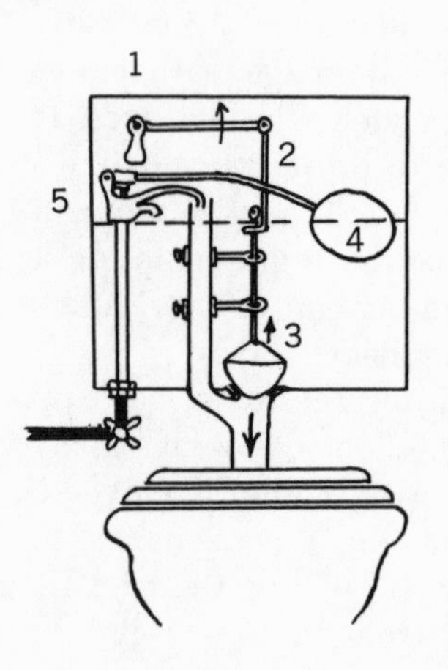

How a toilet tank works. When the flush handle (1) is swung to the right, the flushing arm is lifted as shown by the arrow. (If the handle is moved in the opposite direction, nothing happens.) The wire lift rod (2) then pulls upward on shaft that leads to the ball valve (3) in the base of the tank. As soon as the ball valve rises (as shown by arrow), water surges under it, preventing it from reseating. It doesn't drop back in the valve seat until the tank is empty. As the tank empties, the float valve (4) falls, opening the water inlet valve (5). This shoots water into the tank. The small tube leading into the vertical overflow pipe prevents siphoning, also helps fill bowl. With the rubber ball valve seated in base of tank, and the float dropped to low point, the tank fills again. When the water reaches the preset level, the float has risen enough to shut it off. The flush tank is now ready to flush again. The large lower pipe is called a spud. It leads surge water into the toilet bowl.

When you flip the handle on a toilet flush tank, a metal lever arm on the inner end of the handle shaft lifts a rod that pulls a rubber ball valve out of a large outlet hole in the bottom of the tank. The air-filled rubber ball valve floats upward, so the water in the tank rushes out through a short pipe into the toilet bowl. (The rubber ball valve doesn't float up until you lift it because there's water pressure on top of it, but nothing but air in the empty pipe under it.)

When all the water in the tank has emptied, swirling through the bowl and on down the sewer pipe, the rubber ball valve drops back into the hole again. This seals the outlet so the tank can fill.

When the tank is emptied, a float drops with the water level in the tank, opening a water inlet valve to fill the tank again. As the water entering through this valve fills the tank, the float rises with the water and finally shuts off the valve when the water level reaches the full tank level. If the float valve doesn't shut off completely as it should, the water runs out of the tank through an overflow pipe that leads into the sewer line. This prevents the tank from overflowing. And it also keeps the toilet singing. You hear the water hissing through the not-quite-closed float valve.

You can frequently cure float valve trouble of this type by bending the metal float arm slightly so the float is set a little deeper in the water. This closes the valve at a somewhat lower water level so the water doesn't rise enough to reach the overflow pipe before the supply is shut off.

The other cause of singing is a jangled rubber ball valve (technically it's a stopper ball). If it's a little out of line in its guides, it doesn't plop down into the outlet hole when the tank empties, but lands slightly off center and doesn't seal the outlet. So water keeps on running in through the open float valve and out through the opening the ball valve is supposed to close. And your toilet sings.

This trouble is easily cured by adjusting the guides so the ball valve plops into the outlet hole where it belongs. Take the lid off the tank and pull the ball's guide rod up, then let it drop, and watch where the ball lands. Internal tank details vary, but you'll see the screws that clamp the guides in place. There isn't much room to work so you'll need either a very short screwdriver or a thin dime to loosen the screws for guide adjustment, and to tighten them again. And you'll usually need a flashlight, as most tanks are rust-darkened inside. A few trial adjustments may be needed before the ball hits the bull's-eye.

The guides are mounted on the brass overflow pipe in most tanks, and the pipe is thin-walled. So treat it gently when you make your adjustments. Rough handling can break the pipe at its lower end where its connecting threads weaken it.

In some cases you'll find the ball valve, itself, is in bad shape, sometimes partially collapsed or split. This is an easy fix. All you do is screw it off the threaded end of the guide rod and screw on a new one.

If you have to replace a major part like an overflow pipe or inlet float valve, examine the replacement part carefully where you buy it. (Most hardware stores and all plumbing suppliers stock flush tank parts.) This will give you the clearest picture of the installation details. Buy all washers and gaskets that go with the parts, and have the dealer show you where they go. Periodic variations in these parts make it part of your handyman's technique to ask questions. Wherever possible, it's best to bring the old part with you so you can match it when you buy a replacement. Overflow pipes, for example, are made in several different diameters and lengths. If you can't bring the part along, measure it carefully.

If you've never tackled a plumbing connection or assembly job before, take a good look at *all* the parts and fittings you'll be working on. Then look at new parts of the same type at the hardware store, and notice how they are used. And when you work on any vitreous part of a fixture, like a flush tank, work in such a way that a wrench can't slip and crack the fixture. If you have any doubts, wrap a layer or two of rag around the wrench handle. Naturally, the job has to be done with the water shut off, if any water pipe must be disconnected.

If any major flush tank trouble develops at an off-hour, and the tank has no shut-off valve in its supply pipe, you can usually save the day by tying the float arm in the "up" position with heavy string to stop the flow of water into the tank. This leaves the other fixtures in the house operative.

WHEN THE TOILET OVERFLOWS

Although an overflowing toilet is much more of a shocker than a singing one, it's not as serious a repair job as it looks. As soon as it happens, however, if it's on an upper floor, cover the floor with newspapers, bath mats, towels, or anything absorbent that happens to be handy. This may save you the trouble and expense of refinishing the ceiling underneath it. And you can send your sodden absorbers to the laundry.

If the overflow-causing stoppage is in the toilet itself, it's fairly easy to reach. Typical troublemakers are heavy paper towels (which tend to wad up into a plug) and assorted objects tossed in the bowl by children. The stop-up usually occurs in the inverted

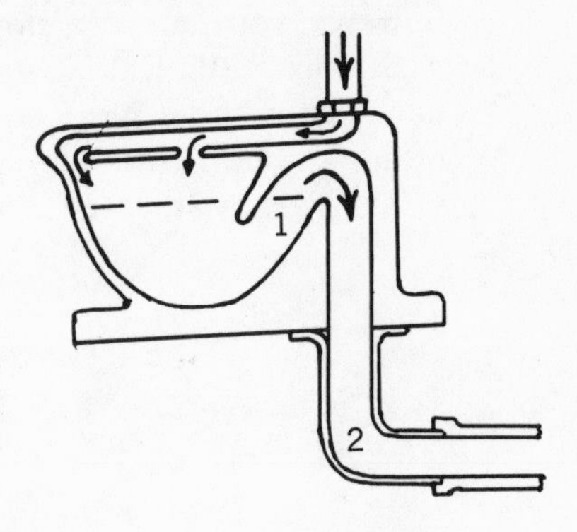

The toilet bowl has built-in inverted U-passage at the rear section to keep bowl water high enough to seal off sewer gases, as shown at (1). This general area is where such objects as toys are likely to lodge and cause blockage. They are often visible. If they pass this point, they may lodge at the next sharp bend (2). The closet auger (a special toilet-type snake) clears either type. Arrows show how water enters, leaves toilet bowl.

U-passage just behind the bowl. In flushing, water rises in the bowl and also in the inverted U-passage, finally flowing over the top of the inverted U and down into the sewer line. As the U-passage is much smaller than the bowl, the blockage usually occurs there. As the water can't escape this way, it simply overflows the bowl. But fortunately it stops when the ball valve drops in the tank.

Handiest tool for clearing a clogged toilet is the closet auger. This is like a short plumber's snake, with a tubular handle long enough to reach to the bottom of the bowl—with the flexible section sliding in ahead of it. A crank at the upper end of the tubular handle lets you rotate the snake as it makes its way through the inverted U-passage behind the bowl.

If you can see any part of the blockage (like a Teddy bear or a plastic rocket ship), you may be able to pull it out without tools, or with a hooked length of coat hanger wire. The closet auger, however, can also break up stoppages several feet beyond the U-channel in the pipe, itself.

REPAIRING LEAKING PIPES

If a water pipe leaks inside of a wall or ceiling, call a plumber. Chances are he can make the repair with less plaster-ripping than you can. If the pipe is in the open where you can get at it, however, you can often stop the leak without much trouble. The easiest fix is the leak along a straight run of pipe. This is most likely to turn up in older houses with galvanized iron pipes. These often develop rusted-through pinholes that drip or spray a little stream when you least expect it. The easiest repair calls for a two-

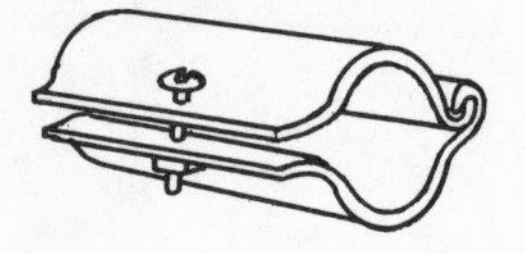

A pipe clamp that seals leaks in water pipes looks like this. Just fit parts together over the leaky point and tighten screw to squeeze the rubber liner against the leak. That stops it.

part pipe leak clamp sized to match the pipe diameter. The two metal halves are joined along one side by a hinge or tongue-and-slot arrangement, and along the other side by two bolts. Each half is lined with a rubber pad. Just remove the bolts to open the clamp. Slip it over the pipe so one of the rubber pads will close against the leak, then close it and tighten it on the pipe with the bolts until the leak stops. The entire job usually takes less than two minutes. If you live in an older home, it pays to keep a few of these quick-fixers on hand to match any pipe that looks suspicious. Large hardware stores and plumbing suppliers have them.

TROUBLE SPOTS IN FROZEN PIPES

If you think of frozen pipes as a strictly rural problem of the distant past, guess again. A pipe can freeze and create a worthwhile commotion even in a modern well-heated house. You may forget to turn off and drain the pipe that feeds the outdoor spigot for your garden hose, for example. And the pipe can freeze and split far enough inside the basement to do a bothersome spray job when it thaws. Or Junior may unhook a basement window to slide one of his carpentry projects out—and forget to close the window. If there's a water pipe just under that window on a zero night, it may be solid by morning.

In general, fittings like pipe elbows, tees, and faucets are likely to split from freezing before the pipe itself splits. But, in any event, remember that once the frozen pipe is thawed, you can expect a stream of water to squirt from any break. If you turn the water off in advance to prevent this, you may waste a lot of thawing time, as you may not know when the job's done. So old-timers usually turn the water *almost* off and turn *on* any faucets blocked by the freeze-up. Then, when the pipe is thawed, water flows from the faucets slowly, and also from any breaks slowly. The rest is a matter of replacing any broken parts—with the water turned off.

SAFE WAY TO THAW

You can use almost any heat source from an infrared bulb to a blowtorch to thaw a frozen pipe. If you don't know exactly where the freeze-up is, open a faucet at the end of the run, and warm the pipe inward from there toward the suspected area. The faucet will signal when you've done the job. Never thaw a pipe from what's likely to be the center of a frozen section, especially with a blowtorch. You can actually melt a section between two ice blocks, generate steam, and blow up the pipe. This can be noisy, expensive, and possibly fatal.

The handiest thawing tool is a propane torch. Feel the pipe as you work along. It needn't be much warmer than body temperature to free a local stoppage.

4

YOU CAN FIX ELECTRICAL THINGS AND LIVE

SOMEWHERE in your house is a main switch that shuts off all the electricity in the place. At the same spot there's also a fuse panel or circuit breaker panel to shut off parts of your house wiring automatically if you plug in more gadgets than the wiring is supposed to handle. Whether you plan to do any electrical repair work or not, it's extremely important that you know where these things are and how to use them. At the very least, this can save you a lot of inconvenience if the lights suddenly go out when a fuse blows. And at the most, it may let you prevent a serious electrical fire if something should ever go seriously haywire in your household electrical system.

LOCATING THE MAIN SWITCH

If you've just moved into your house, get the builder to send somebody around to show you where the main switch and fuse panel are and how to use them. If you've been in the house for quite a while, have the electric power company send someone to tell you the facts of electrical living. All this in case you don't know from beans about electricity. Under no condition should you go around flipping electrical levers or unscrewing things from basement fuse panels unless you're *sure* of what you're doing. When you know the ropes, however, there's nothing even slightly dangerous about it.

In some houses the main switch is a steel box about candy box size with a steel handle sticking out of one side and the words "on" and "off" printed at the two positions the handle can take. You'll usually find this mounted on a plywood panel somewhere on the basement wall just below the outside point where the electric wires lead into your house from the power lines on the street poles. Another type of main switch is the pull-out block variety that's a part of some fuse panels. This is actually a removable plastic block labeled "Main." It usually has a shiny little handle on it like the kind you see on a toy suitcase. You use this to pull the block completely out of the fuse panel to shut everything off. When the block is removed, the juice is turned off. But

This is what a fuse panel looks like. Have a professional show you how it works.

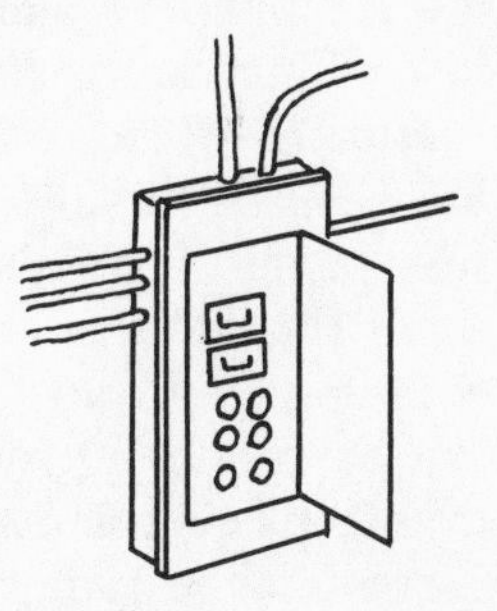

don't try sticking your fingers in the hole the block came out of. Electricity still gets that far. In this type of setup there's usually another almost identical block labeled "Range." When this is pulled out, it shuts off the juice to the electric range in the kitchen (if you have an electric range) or to some other gadget connected to it. But it doesn't shut off everything. So be sure you pull the correct one (or pull both) if you want everything shut off. If anybody with electrical know-how shows you these things the first time, you can't make a mistake.

WHEN A FUSE BLOWS

Fuses shut off the electricity automatically when too much current begins to flow through the wiring, as when you plug in too many electrical gadgets. They're necessary because any current flowing through wires tends to warm them up a little. And too much current can make them so hot the insulation catches fire. To keep this from happening, the fuse contains a short piece of special alloy wire that heats up and melts with much less current than ordinary wire. So as soon as the electrical current load gets big enough to approach the danger level, the fuse wire melts, breaks, and shuts off the whole business. You have a blown fuse, and your lights go out in the section of the house that's connected through that fuse.

When a fuse blows it's usually easy to tell why. If it blew just as you switched on a lamp, that lamp may have been defective or it may have added the final straw to the electrical load. Either way, unplug the lamp before you replace the fuse, or the new fuse will probably blow as soon as you put it in.

How to replace a fuse. After disconnecting whatever seems to have caused the fuse to blow, take a flashlight and head for your fuse panel. If it's above a cement floor (like a basement floor), there should be a little platform of dry boards in front of it. Standing on a cement floor, especially if it happens to be damp, can be very dangerous when you're doing any electrical work—even replacing a fuse. Before you touch the fuse, shut off the current at the main switch, whatever kind it is. You can usually tell which fuse is blown by looking at the little window in the

A fuse looks like this. If it's 15 amps or less, it will have a hexagonal window, as shown, or some other prominent hexagonal feature—such as the outer rim. Higher amperage fuses don't have hexagonal features.

fuse cap. Sometimes you can see the fuse wire melted through. Or the window may be blackened. One way or another, the blown fuse nearly always looks quite different from the good ones. To replace it, just unscrew it and screw in another *just like it.* The blown fuse will have its ampere rating marked on it—usually 15 or 20 amps. Then turn on the juice again and you're back in business. *Never* replace a fuse with one that has a higher rating marked on it. If you do this, the fuse won't blow when it's supposed to and your wiring will get hot instead. This can easily prove a roundabout way of burning down your house.

After you replace a fuse, always throw away the blown one. Otherwise you may get it mixed up with the spares (which should be kept near the fuse panel) and end up sometime replacing a blown fuse with another blown fuse. You can save yourself some trouble, too, by pasting a list of the fuse socket numbers on the back of the panel door along with the specific rooms they supply. Then if the lights go out in any particular room, you know just which fuse needs replacing.

When you know which rooms or outlets are fed by a given fuse, you can also avoid blowing the fuse by simply avoiding an overload. As a handy rule of the thumb, just add two zeros to the ampere rating marked on the fuse. For a 15 ampere fuse, the result would thus be 1500. That's how many watts the fuse can supply before blowing out. So a 15 ampere fuse can handle ten 150 watt bulbs, or the equivalent, before the lights go out. (Actually, it can do somewhat better than that, but the two-zero rule keeps you on the safe side.)

HOW TO OPERATE A CIRCUIT BREAKER

If your house is equipped with circuit breakers instead of fuses, things are even easier for you electrically. The circuit breakers are mounted on a panel just like fuses, but they look like ordinary wall switches—in rows. There's one for each branch circuit in the house, just as with fuses. If something happens that would blow a fuse, the circuit breaker simply flips into "tripped" position like a switch opened by some invisible hand. This shuts off the electricity to the part of the house involved just as a blown fuse would do. But to get things going again, you don't have to remove anything or replace anything. You just flip the circuit breaker to "reset" position and it pops back to "on." Some must be pushed back to "on." If you want to use the circuit breaker to turn off the electricity to a part of the house so you can work on the wiring, you merely flip the little handle to "off."

Not all circuit breaker panels have a separate main breaker that turns everything off at once, like a main switch. If the house

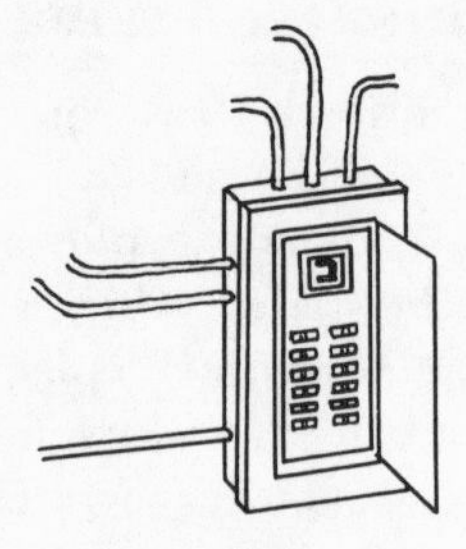

A circuit breaker panel looks like a fuse panel but has rows of toggle-switch (like wall switch) handles instead of round fuses. You don't have to replace anything when lights go out—just flip the toggle.

Some circuit breaker toggle levers are mounted to work vertically, others move horizontally. The relative lever positions are the same. In the vertical example illustrated the normal (on) position is at the top. If the circuit is "overloaded," as by a faulty appliance, the circuit breaker "breaks" the circuit (like a blown fuse) and simultaneously flips the toggle lever to the "tripped" position. To turn it on again you must first push it all the way down to the "reset" position, then push it up to the "on" position. If you get to the circuit breaker panel quickly (after the lights go out) you may have to wait two or three minutes for the thermal mechanism to cool. Until it does, it won't turn the lights on again no matter what you do with the lever. If you simply want to turn off the circuit (as in preparation for replacement of a switch or outlet) you push the lever to the "off" position. Most circuit breakers have labels indicating the different positions, but old ones may have worn, unreadable lettering. If the print is illegible let a power company man explain the positions. Some breakers snap back to "on" position from "reset." Most now have to be pushed. Because of minor variations, your best bet if in doubt is to let a pro show you the right way to work the thing.

ON

TRIPPED (BLOWN)

TURNED OFF

RESET

is small enough so that you can turn off all the separate branch circuit breakers with not more than six movements of your hand, it need not have a separate main breaker. If it takes more than six hand movements to shut everything off, the panel must have a separate breaker that turns off everything at once. Be sure you find out how to turn off individual branch circuits and the whole business, too, before you do any electrical fix-it jobs.

PRECAUTIONS TO TAKE

It's easy and safe to make simple house wiring repairs if you follow a few basic rules, and *always* shut off the current at the *main switch* before you touch the wiring. If it's very important to leave the current turned on in some other parts of the house while you make your repair, you can unscrew the fuse that supplies the section of the house you'll be working on. But be *absolutely sure* you unscrew the correct fuse and that the current is definitely *off* in the wiring you'll be working on. And be sure no well-meaning soul turns the juice on while you're working. Once you've taken these precautions, you can work safely. You can't be electrocuted by wires that have no electricity in them.

REPLACING A SWITCH

People replace wall switches for many reasons. Sometimes the switch goes on the bum and just won't work. Or you may want to change from a snap switch (that clicks so loudly the baby starts yelling in the middle of the night) to a silent type. Or you may want to install one of the fancy new dimmer switches that lets you turn your lights up or down gradually to any brightness level you want, the way they do it in the theater. All these different switches fit in the same standard wall switch box that's already in your wall. All you have to do is disconnect two wires from the old switch and connect the same two wires to the new one.

First, turn off the current at the main switch. Then remove the screws from the top and bottom of the switch cover plate on the wall, and then lift off the cover plate. This exposes the switch itself. You can see it's held in the metal wall box by two more little screws, one at the top, another at the bottom. Take the screws out and you can pull the switch several inches out of the box with the wires still connected to it. The extra wire length is left there for this purpose. You'll notice that the wires are connected to two brass screws on the switch. Turn these screws counterclockwise to loosen them (they won't come all the way out), and slip the wires out from under the screw heads. Then put the old switch aside and connect the wires to the new switch just as they were connected to the old one. Just be sure the loops in the ends of the wires are in the same position as before—so the loops will tend to close as you tighten the screws on them.

Fasten the new switch to the box just the same as the old one. The screw holes will match because the whole works is standardized as to threads, spacing, and just about everything else. So the cover plate goes on exactly the same as before, too. After that, just turn on the main switch and your new wall switch is ready for action. The job is actually that simple.

There are a few important points to keep in mind when you buy a new switch, however. If it's a mercury switch, one end of it will be marked "up" or "top." Be sure this end is up when you mount it in the box. Otherwise it won't work. Mercury switches are just one type of silent switch. There are mechanical silent switches, too. These can be mounted in any position.

INSTALLATION OF DIMMER TYPES

Dimmer switches are mostly of the electronic type, with exactly the same kind of connections as ordinary switches. So you have just the usual two connections to make. (There's a transformer type that's connected differently. If you want to use one of these, get complete instructions where you buy it. There may be some extra wiring involved.)

What the dimmer switches can do varies according to the type. One form is called a bulb extender. It has only one setting—dim—plus "off." But it increases the operating life of the bulb by forty to one-hundred-fifty times—which means an ordinary bulb will last from four to fifteen years. This is the least expensive dimmer switch. Use it for things like gatepost lamps where bulb replacement means work. To get the amount of light you want, just use a larger bulb.

The two-stage dimmer is slightly higher in price and provides full light, dim light (about 30 per cent full), and off. This is handy in many parts of the house, especially in children's bedrooms.

The half-range dimmer costs still more. You can turn it from "off" to "on" at low level, then gradually all the way up to half brilliance. From there it jumps to full brilliance in one step. This is a good one for any room where you use television.

The full-range dimmer tops the price list and provides the whole show. Turn it from "off" to "on" at the bottom of the dimming range, then gradually all the way up to full. You can, of course, set any dimmer at any level you like and leave it there. Some also have double-acting knobs that let you turn the lights on and off at any level you select—so you don't have to adjust the lighting level each time you turn the lights on. Whatever the dimmer type, use it *only* for lights unless it's approved for other purposes.

One more tip on bulb life in case you'd like to extend it *without* a dimmer switch. If you plan a vacation trip and want to leave a light burning in your house to foil intruders, simply buy a 230 volt bulb and screw it into one of your regular 120 volt lamps. You can get one of these from any electrical supplier. As it will burn at approximately half voltage, it will last for years. A 150 watt size will actually use only about 50 watts, and will provide a warm, mellow light throughout a fair-sized room.

HOW TO REPLACE AN OUTLET

If the cord plugs have a habit of falling out of an outlet, the chances are you need a new outlet receptacle. (The receptacle is the gismo you stick the plug into.) You start the replacement job by shutting off the current at the main switch, as usual. Then you take off the cover plate. This is held by a single screw in the center, not by two screws like a switch plate. The receptacle is held to the metal wall box the same as a switch, by a little screw at each end. Remove these screws and you can pull the receptacle out of the box with the wires still connected, just as you can pull out a switch. But there's an extra point to watch for about the wiring. One of the wires is *black,* the other *white.* (Both wires running to a switch are black if the original job was done correctly.) You'll also note that the *black* wire connects to the *brass* terminal screw of the receptacle, and the *white* wire connects to the *chrome* terminal screw. When you replace the old receptacle

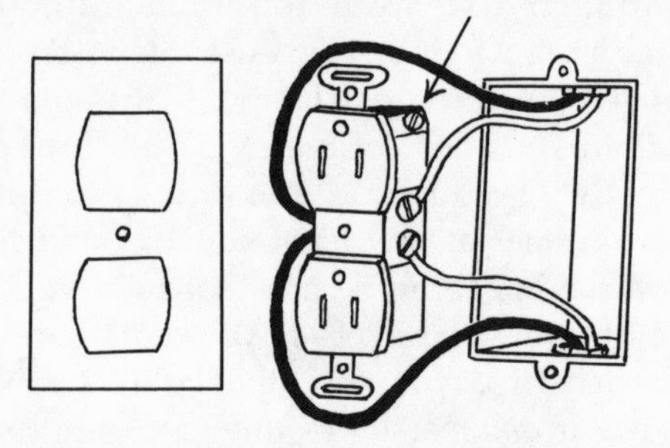

Electrical wall receptacles look like this when you pull them out of the box. Some have only two wires (one black, one white), others have four (two blacks and two whites). The black ones are always on one side, the whites on the other. Arrow shows modern grounding terminal, which is sprayed green. This may or may not have wire connected to it, depending on the locality. Always reconnect it as it was. Black wires always go to brass terminals, white ones to chrome.

with a new one, connect the new one in *exactly* the same way—*black* wire to *brass* terminal, *white* wire to *chrome.* That's all there is to it, but it's *extremely* important. Severe shock hazards can result if you get them reversed.

When you're replacing an existing outlet, you may be able to add a little convenience. Instead of the usual duplex receptacle that takes just two plugs, you can now get triplex and quadruplex models that fit in the same old wall box but take three or four plugs, respectively. Wiring connections are just the same as for the plain old duplex.

About grounding outlets

These outlets are the ones with three holes instead of the usual two, to take plugs with three prongs instead of two. The third prong connects to a third wire in the plug-in cord. This connects the outside shell of power tools and appliances to the grounding wire of your house wiring system, and gives you extra shock protection in case anything goes wrong.

This type of outlet is required by regulation in all *new* wiring, but it isn't required for replacement jobs. So you can use the old two-slot type of receptacle if that's what you now have. And it's usually better not to switch from the old style to the new style unless you're sure the house wiring is suited to the new outlets. (Many old house wiring systems lack the necessary grounding wires for the new outlets.)

If your house already has the three-hole outlets you must replace them (when necessary) with the same kind. You'll notice that these have a third terminal screw on them—sprayed green for identification. In some localities this terminal is connected to a green wire that is connected to a screw in the metal box at its other end. This is called a grounding jumper wire. If it's there, connect it to the new receptacle in the same way. Connect the black and white wires as described earlier.

If you don't find the green jumper wire (some localities don't require it), there's no need to add it to the new receptacle. The national electrical code advises the jumper, but local codes take precedence over the national one. So if they don't like the jumper wire, you don't use it.

HOW CODES AND PERMITS HELP YOU

The *National Electrical Code* is a little fat book of safe wiring rules compiled over the years by insurance people and wiring experts. It aims to keep both professionals and amateurs from hooking up house wiring in cockeyed ways that can electrocute somebody or set the whole neighborhood on fire. For example, it tells you just what type of insulated cable you can use in damp places and what kind you can't use. And it tells you that all wire-to-wire connections must be made inside of approved wiring boxes. You can't just hook a couple of wires together and leave them dangling from the ceiling. In short, it's just a good collection of common sense wiring advice. It doesn't have the force of law, however, unless the local town fathers make it a part of local regulations. When they do this, as they do in most communities, they often add some more rules of their own—and there's no rule that says these can't be stupid. Don't be surprised, for example, if the local code agrees with the national code and contradicts it, too. Fortunately, the national code does not say a homeowner can't work on the wiring of his own home, and most local codes agree. In some areas, for example, the electrical inspector's office even provides pamphlets to tell the homeowner how to avoid wiring errors in do-it-yourself wiring work.

Where there's a local code, you'll usually need a permit to do any major wiring job like adding new outlets, or wiring a newly finished attic. The fee for the permit is usually reasonable, and covers the cost of a visit by the wiring inspector. If all's well, he approves the job and that's all there is to it. If you've goofed, he'll tell you what the goof is and how to correct it. He isn't the ogre he's often painted. In fact, part of the inspector's job is telling people in advance (if they ask him) how to avoid wiring blunders. So if you have wiring plans in mind, get in touch with the inspector ahead of time and get a copy of the local code plus all the dope on permits and fees.

5

HOW TO FIX APPLIANCES WITHOUT WRECKING THEM

UNLESS you've had some mechanical experience, leave major appliance repairs to the pros. If you try the job and bungle it, you'll probably leave the thing in worse shape than it was in when you started. But there are some things you can fix without yelling for help, and you can save time and money by doing it.

WHEN THE VACUUM CLEANER FAILS

In general, when something doesn't work, look for the obvious. (Repairmen have actually been called because somebody forgot to plug something in.) The vacuum cleaner, for example, is prone to some trivial ailments that are easily spotted. If it drones along pleasantly, but stops sucking, it usually has one of these easy-cure troubles. First, check the bag. It's probably been there longer than you think. Usually, however, you'll find the cause of the no-suck trouble in the hose or its fittings. A narrow-slit carpet-cleaning attachment can be blocked by a relatively small dust crawler. Just yank out whatever's clogging it. If nothing seems clogged, disconnect the hose from everything, cup your hands over one end, and blow through it. If it's blocked inside, a skinny mop handle will usually shove the blockage near enough to one end to permit fishing it out with a hook-ended piece of coat hanger wire. Just don't punch a hole in the hose.

If the hose isn't blocked, look for a split in it. This is likeliest near the ends, where the hose joins the metal tube ends. If you find a split, you can fix it well enough to finish the day's cleaning job in most cases by patching it over with a lot of sticky tape and treating it tenderly. Cellulose or masking tape will do.

In the course of vacuum cleaner trouble diagnosis, it also pays to keep in mind the kind of problems that may make you look like an idiot. Some cleaners, for example, have little valves that you open for special jobs. If you leave them open, the thing won't work on other jobs. Other types can be hooked up backwards for paint spraying. Then they blow instead of sucking. If you find you've absent-mindedly pulled one of these boners, just set things right and shut up about it. You'll be the only one who knows just what kind of a nut you are.

STEAM IRONS THAT DON'T STEAM

Irons that don't steam may or may not be within the novice's fix-it abilities. If the iron has been used at high heat, it may have lost its water supply overly fast through spitting. Some irons are more subject to this than others. If this is the trouble, no repair is needed. Just water.

If the iron is plugged in, turned on, but cold, you can hope the trouble is in the cord. That's something you can fix yourself in an emergency when you can't buy a new one. One of the best ways to test an appliance cord (and lots of other electrical things) is with a neon test light. This is a little neon tube light usually a little smaller than a cigarette, with a pair of insulated wires sticking out of it with prods on the ends. The prods are metal prongs with insulated handles on them where they join the wires. To test the iron cord (if it's the kind you can remove from the iron), first remove it from the iron, then plug it into a wall outlet. Push one of the test light prods into each hole that would normally slip on to the attaching prongs of the iron. With both test light prods in the holes, the test light will glow red if the cord is OK. If it doesn't glow, unplug the cord and take apart the attaching plug at the iron end—if it's the kind that comes apart. Usually it's made in two halves held together by a pair of long skinny screws with nuts on the other end. Don't lose the screws or the nuts. Inside you'll see the actual wires. Look for a broken wire close to one of the terminal screws to which the wires connect. As the insulation on ironing cord wires is surrounded by stranded asbestos, you may have to poke through some fluff to make your inspection.

If you find a broken wire, remove the broken end from the terminal screw. Then strip off insulation from the end of the wire itself, so there's enough bare wire to loop around the terminal screw and reconnect. Then clip off the ends of the other wires, one at a time, bare the ends in the same way, and reconnect them. This clipping of the unbroken wires is usually necessary to keep uneven lengths from causing bunching, crimping, or straining of the wires. There's lots of variation in cord fittings, of course, and the one you have may not quite match up to the repair just described. But if you disconnect only one wire at a time and reconnect it before disconnecting another, you can't make a mistake in connections. When the job's done, however, take a very careful look at all connections to make sure no stray strand of any wire is loose. A single straggler from one wire, touching another, can cause a direct short circuit and a blown fuse.

The plug at the other end of the ironing cord is less likely to be the cause of trouble, though it sometimes is. This one is easy to repair if it can be repaired at all. If it has screw terminals, look for a broken wire as before, and make the repair in the same way.

If your iron is a type with the cord permanently attached and there's nothing wrong with the cord plug, don't try taking the iron apart to look for trouble. If you're a novice, you'll probably make more trouble than you had in the first place and probably lose some little parts in the process. Just take the iron to a pro and get it fixed right.

WASHING MACHINE BREAKDOWNS

Washing machines, both for clothes and dishes, can also act up occasionally, like all mechanical gadgets. And if you're a nonprofessional, you shouldn't attempt any major operations. Your best bet is to have the owner's manual on hand, however, so you can cure the minor ills without yelling for help that you have to pay for. In the absence of the manual, check all accessible strainers—especially the lint traps. In some types, too, you may hear a motor whirring merrily when nothing else is moving. In this event, if you can get a look at the internal machinery, you'll probably find a V-belt broken. This is simply a reinforced rubber pulley belt that's supposed to carry power from one pulley wheel to another (the way a bicycle chain works on a bike). If you find one of these broken or shredded somewhere inside or under the machine, take it with you to the appliance dealer and get a new one to match it. You can usually put it on yourself.

When the washing machine overflows

If you didn't pay much attention when your washer was installed, there's a chance that you may sometime be surprised to find a torrent of water cascading across the floor from somewhere under the machine. While this isn't common, it's more than a little disconcerting when it happens. But it's seldom hard to cure. In the typical case, it's caused by the slip-off of a short length of hose that connects the machine to the plumbing behind it. Happily, there's usually a spigot-type valve at the end of the connecting pipe. If you can pull the machine out a little, you can dangle an arm in back of it and shut off the valve. After that it's just a matter of wiggling the machine out far enough to permit reconnecting the hose. And be sure the metal hose clamp holds it tightly to the pipe.

REPAIRING OR REPLACING LAMP SOCKETS

Lamps that won't light are almost always a simple enough job for a novice to handle successfully. The same applies to lamps that flicker and make sputters on the radio. The first step, of course, is diagnosis. Make sure the bulb is in tight. Make sure the cord plug is the same. Then try a new bulb anyway. Sometimes a broken filament in a bulb welds itself partially, then makes a poor contact. The result can be flickers of the bulb and sputters of the radio. If a new bulb cures your lamp trouble, stop there.

If your checkup shows the trouble to be in the lamp itself, the bulb socket, the switch, or both are likely to be ailing. Disconnect the lamp by pulling the plug out of the wall outlet. Then unscrew the bulb, and look down in the bulb socket. In some types you'll see two tiny little screw heads, one on each side, down in the bottom. If so, try tightening them with a very small screwdriver. This sometimes cures the trouble. Take a look at the metal tab in the dead center of the socket bottom. If it's blackened or pitted, scrape it clean with the tip of a knife blade or with a small, sharp screwdriver. This is one of the electrical contacts that supplies juice to the bulb. Cleaning it sometimes cures lamp trouble.

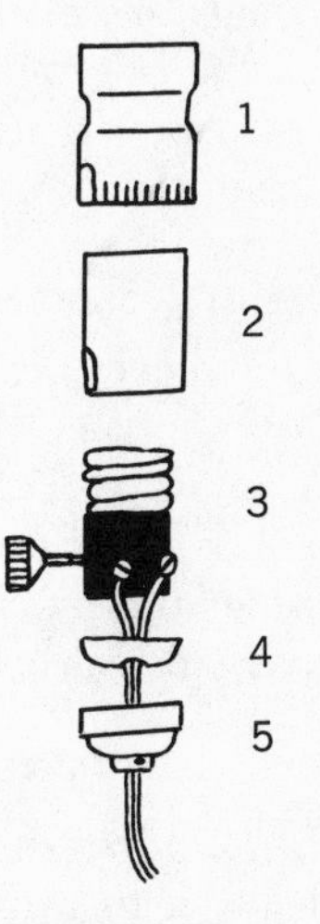

A lamp socket looks like this (switch type) when you take it apart for connecting. A metal shell (1) is at the top. An insulating fiber inner shell (2) and switch and socket body (3) are next. An insulating fiber inner cap (4) is next with metal outer cap (5) below it. Wires are connected as shown. All parts snap together.

If neither of the easy cures above does the trick, try a complete new socket, just like the one already in the lamp. If it has a switch (as most lamps have), get a socket with the same kind of switch—push-button, turn-knob, pull-chain, etc. You can buy all types at any hardware store and most dime stores.

To remove the old socket, first look closely around its metal shell for the spot marked "press." Then squeeze the shell with your hand so that your thumb presses hard at that spot. If you're a hard squeezer, you can then lift the socket shell out of the metal cap that forms its base. You'll notice that the shell is lined with a tubular fiber insulator, and that the metal base cap has a cup-shaped one, too. Also, you can now see the wires and the terminals to which they connect. Simply disconnect the wires and lift out the old switch and socket unit. At this point you can also remove the base cap, sliding it up and off the wires. But if your new socket is a matching one, you can leave the old cap alone, as the shell of the new socket will fit right into it anyway. Just connect the wires to the terminals on the new switch and socket unit in the same way they were connected to the old one. There are just two wires and two terminals. One of the terminal screws is brass, the other chrome. If the lamp wires are black and white, they connect black to brass, white to chrome. The way most lamp cord plugs are made, they fit into wall outlets any old way and mix up the color coding, anyway, but it's a good idea to follow it in your connections just the same. If there's no way to tell one wire from the other, of course, all you can do is connect one to each terminal screw.

Finish the job by slipping the socket shell with its insulating liner down over the switch and socket unit, and into the base cap. It snaps in place. Throw away the old inside unit that didn't work, but save the extra shells and caps, new or old. They can come in handy if some other shell or cap gets damaged. Once the new inner unit is connected and the shell snapped in place, the lamp is ready for business again.

FIXING APPLIANCES WITH ELECTRIC MOTORS

When an electric motor won't start, shut it off immediately. If you leave it turned on, you may burn out an important part of it—depending on how the motor is wired. If it's a little motor like the kind on a small electric fan, it may simply need a little oil. Look for little holes marked "oil." These are usually near the ends of the motor, where the shaft sticks out. If you can't find any such hole, put a drop or two of light oil (like 3-in-1) on the shaft, close to the points where it comes out of the motor. The oil will seep into the bearings. If you can turn the shaft by hand, as in turning the blades of a fan, do it before you turn on the juice. After a few turns you'll often be able to feel the thing ease up and turn much more easily. This sticky shaft kind of trouble results from old oil getting gummy in a long-neglected motor.

When a bigger motor won't start (like the ones that run table saws), look for something jamming it—often something stuck in the thing the motor is supposed to run. And look for a bad connection in the motor's plug-in cord. A broken plug or a partially broken connection can do it. Try turning the shaft of the motor, too (with power off). If it turns easily, there's another trick you can try. Wrap some heavy cord around the shaft so that when you pull it, the motor will spin in the direction it normally runs. Then turn on the juice and yank the cord to spin the motor. If the motor keeps on running after you spin it, you need some professional help. It may have a burned out starter winding or some related trouble. You can't fix this yourself without real know-how. Get a definite estimate on the repair job. You may find you can buy a new motor for less.

Foiling a motor-killer. There are two common causes of burned-out starter windings. One of the sneakiest is lower-than-normal voltage in the power lines that bring electricity to your house. This sometimes shows up after the lights go out during an electrical (lightning) storm. Your lights come on—but dimly. Your refrigerator tries to start but just keeps humming and grunting. In winter this dim light condition gets your oil burner doing the same hum and grunt act. When this happens, *shut everything off*. Starter windings in a motor are intended to spin the motor for just a few seconds to get it up to the speed where its regular windings (wire coils) can take over and keep it running. So the starter windings are made of thin wire. If they have to keep laboring, they heat up and burn out. Low voltage can ruin them. So can a heavy load applied to a motor while it's starting.

Motors that blow fuses. If some fairly big electric motor around the house occasionally blows a fuse just as it starts, the chances are it's a cinch to take care of. Many motors use around ten times as much current getting started as they do running. So you simply buy a time-lag fuse to replace the blown fuse. Be *sure* it has the same ampere rating as the old fuse—it doesn't need to have more, and it *should not* have more. This type of fuse doesn't blow out as soon as it gets hit with an electrical overload, but waits for a second or two. By that time the motor has reached full speed and is no longer causing an overload, so the fuse doesn't blow out. But you still have complete overload protection. If the overload ever lasts more than a second or two, the fuse will blow like any other fuse.

DO'S AND DON'T'S FOR GAS APPLIANCES

If you have a kitchen range or other appliances that use natural or bottled gas, you're not likely to smell the stuff unless something is wrong. In fact, these gases usually have no smell of their own. The smell is put in chemically by the utility company just to serve as a signal that something is leaking or that a pilot light has gone out. And it's extremely important that you know what to do if your nose picks up this particular danger signal. Because our noses vary a lot in their sensitivity to smells (and a cold or hay fever can make matters worse), you can't be sure just how much gas the smell indicates. So play it safe and assume there's a lot of gas leaking.

First of all, *don't* do anything that can cause a spark or flame. Don't use any electrical switches and don't plug or unplug any electrical cords. And don't thoughtlessly switch on your kitchen exhaust fan to pull out the gas. If the pilot light is out, *don't* try to light it. You want no spark or flame until the gas has been cleared out. Just open the kitchen windows and any other windows that will help, and get out of the kitchen.

If your phone is in a room not affected by the gas, use it to phone the utility company immediately. But don't use a kitchen phone for the purpose. If your only phone is in a gas-laden room, go to one of your neighbors to phone. The utility company will give your gas-leak call precedence over other service work. All this is plainly precautionary. Gas leaks don't occur often and are seldom serious. When one occurs in your home or in an appliance in your home, find out from the service man who repairs it just what caused it. And find out how to avoid it. There's too much variation in homes and appliances to allow any general complete repair advice. But you'll never go wrong by treating a gas leak with a little too much respect.

WHAT TO DO WHEN YOUR REFRIGERATOR WON'T OPEN

If your refrigerator has a mechanical door catch instead of a magnetic one you can face a nerve-wracking problem if the door handle ever happens to break off. And it happens. In this predicament you can't open the door even by apelike pulling tactics. But don't panic. Look calmly at the broken part of the handle and also at the corresponding broken part still remaining in the handle hole of the refrigerator door. If you move the broken handle the way you always did to open the door you can visualize the way it would move the broken part in the door. And just about every time you'll find there's a way to use a screwdriver to pry that in-the-door broken part so it releases the catch and lets the door open.

Once the door is open look for ways to *prevent* the broken catch from working. Usually there's a recess in the rim around the door, and this is what the catch tongue pops into. A piece of tin scissored from a can and flattened, can cover the hole. Stick it in place with plenty of cellulose tape. Then you can push the door shut and stick it shut with a couple of strips of the same kind of tape. About 8 or 10 inches of tape across the door seam can close the refrigerator door like a Christmas package until you do something better. Just peel off the tape to open the door.

To make a permanent repair open the door and take a good look to see how you can get the broken catch out. Sometimes there's a plate in the edge of the door with shiny screws holding it. If it's there take it out. If the whole busted works comes out with it, relax. That's the easy way. If there is no catch plate you may have to take the whole inside surface of the door off. This looks like an awful job but it usually isn't. Just remove the big, shiny, very obvious screws, and get it over with. (It's interesting to see what's inside the door, anyway.)

Try to replace the handle and catch mechanism through your refrigerator dealer. If this can't be done, however, there's an easy answer. If your budget is tight there's no sense in replacing the whole costly refrigerator just because the door won't work.

Instead, rig the thing with the same kind of magnetic catch your hardware store sells for kitchen cabinets. These things are made in two parts—one with a magnet in it, the other with a simple little steel catch strip. If your refrigerator is *not* finished inside with vitreous enamel (a fused-on glasslike layer) just bore holes where necessary and fasten the magnetic catch parts in place with sheet metal screws. Your hardware dealer can tell you the correct size twist drill to use for the screw size.

If you're facing vitreous enamel (which is really excellent inside a refrigerator) you have a choice of catch-fastening methods. You can buy a tiny grinding wheel on a shaft at your hardware store. You want the kind used in high speed hand grinders. In your power drill (if you have one) this can chew down to the metal so you can drill the necessary sheet metal screw holes. (If you try drilling through vitreous enamel otherwise you'll chip and crack it in messy style.)

If this procedure is too much trouble you can actually glue the magnetic catch parts in place. First, fasten each one with short screws to a piece of plywood (preferably exterior grade) about one and a half to two-inch square. Then glue the plywood squares to the refrigerator and the door. You can use medium grit aluminum oxide paper to roughen the surfaces they'll be glued to. (You'll find complete descriptions of the types of glue that suit this purpose in Chapter 14. Rubber base, Buna-N, acrylic, and epoxy.) The Buna-N (like Pliobond) is the least expensive of the very quick setting types, but it calls for covering or wrapping refrigerator contents until its aroma fades. The acrylic 3-Ton Adhesive (get it at big boatyards), also very fast setting, costs more, but smells and tastes like some of the stuff dentists use to fill your teeth—because it has much the same formula and super strength. You can also use epoxy or rubber base types. Let the circumstances be your guide.

General tips. If you're removing a broken catch unit look out for things that pop in your face. The catches have springs in them, and sometimes shower you with parts when you take out the final screw. They don't all do it, but be careful.

When it comes to mounting a magnetic catch to replace an old and broken mechanical catch, it often helps if you first mount the magnetic catches with cellulose tape—and mark their position with pencil. These catches have to come in actual contact to get a good grip. The tape lets you shift them until they do. Then, they may grip hard enough to pull the tape loose. That's when the pencil mark tells you where to put the parts for final assembly.

As refrigerators vary in contour around the inside of the door you may have to use your brain a little in adapting the new catches to their surroundings, and arranging for them to meet when the door is closed. But a little brainwork won't do any harm. If you're in the habit of using your brain you won't even notice it. And if you're not, you may get to like it.

EMERGENCY REPAIRS TO HEATING ELEMENTS

Burned-out heating elements can turn up in just about anything from a toaster or a hair dryer to a kitchen oven. If you can be leisurely about fixing it, the best bet is to take the part that contains the element to an electrical supply dealer so he can match a new one to the old one. All this applies mainly to the coiled resistance wire type, as the rod type seldom burns out—but you're not likely to find it in smaller appliances.

If you have to make a quick emergency repair of one of these things, to finish roasting a holiday turkey, for instance, first disconnect the appliance or shut off the juice at the main switch. Then get at the burned-out element—as conveniently as possible. The elements in ranges and wall ovens are usually removable, in many cases on a pull-out-plug basis. (You should know about this if you bought the appliance.) And an oven is about the only burnout likely to present a real emergency. When the element unit is cool and out where you can look at it, examine the coiled heating element from one end to the other, looking for a break. A light pencil-prodding is helpful, as the broken ends often remain so perfectly aligned that they don't show. If you find a break somewhere along the run of the resistance wire, between connections, straighten out half an inch of each broken end, using pliers, and clean the straightened portions with fine sandpaper. This takes off the oxide coating so you can get a good electrical contact when you reconnect the break. If there's room, the best way to join the broken ends is with a short bolt and nut. Just loop the cleaned wire ends under the head of a round-head bolt, and tighten the nut to hold them together. The loops should be made in a clockwise direction (so tightening the nut will tighten the loops), and a flat washer should be used between the nut and the wire—if you happen to have a flat washer to fit. Otherwise forget it, but tighten the nut carefully so as not to mess up the wire. Repaired this way, the element is likely to last for months. Just be sure the nut and bolt don't come in contact with any part of the metal frame of the unit.

When the break in the heating element wire is close to one of the original terminal screws, the whole repair job is a lot easier. Just loosen the terminal screw and remove the broken wire end. Then straighten out about half or three quarters of an inch of the wire with pliers, clean it as described previously, and loop it under the terminal screw. Tighten the screw and you have a long-lasting repair.

After any heating element repair, however, it's a good idea to follow up by replacing the entire wire element. Take the whole unit with you to the electrical supply dealer so he can match the wattage of the new wire to the wattage of the old one.

EXTINGUISHING AN OVEN FIRE

The blazing oven is another appliance problem, although it doesn't usually indicate anything is wrong with the appliance. But it calls for a mighty quick remedy. It usually shows up first as smoke trailing out of the oven vent. If, as is usually the case, the broiler is in action, the whole kitchen may be full of smoke. If you open the oven door, all the blazes in hell seem to sail out at you. In this event, try to hang on to your nonchalance and just shut the oven door again. The chances are the big, beautiful sirloin inside isn't ruined, the house won't burn down, and the entire mess isn't as bad as it looks.

First, turn off the broiler. Then yank the top off your biggest salt container. Next open the oven again and slide the broiler rack and the steak out a little with a carving fork or some other long utensil that won't burn and doesn't make you reach in so close you get spattered with fiery fat. (Fiery fat can set your clothing afire.) Then *pile* on the salt by the fistful—at the points the flames are coming from. This salt business is a sort of old wives' tale, but it works if you have plenty of the stuff. It doesn't act chemically by creating some fancy fire-smothering gas. It simply stifles the fire by covering it up and shutting off its air supply—like a load of sand. But it's better than sand from the culinary standpoint because you can wash it off, and if a few grains remain they won't chip your teeth. Whatever you do, *don't* throw water on the fire. This blasts into steam, floats and spatters blazing grease all over the place, and can give you some very nasty burns and possibly set the kitchen on fire.

Actually things cool off surprisingly fast with the broiler turned off and salt piled on the conflagration. Everything usually is under complete control in a minute or two. But even with the fire out, you're likely to have a case of jitters. Just remember it's not anywhere near as horrible as it looks.

In the rare event that you can't put the fire out (most unlikely), shove the whole works back in the oven and shut the door—also the oven vent if possible. This, at least, keeps your private inferno locked up where it can do the least harm until the fire trucks arrive.

Saving the sirloin after the fire is also important. While this book deals only with the mechanical and hard-goods aspects of kitchen blundering, you certainly ought to know how to reclaim your soot-covered dinner if you can—and you usually can. Begin by kicking everybody out of the kitchen. People love a spectacle, and you'll find them wandering around the scene trying to look like a rescue team in a hurricane. So put the biggest nut in command, hand him a bottle, tell him to calm the passengers, avoid a panic, and mix a drink. But not in the kitchen.

Then hoist your smoldering beef over to the sink drainboard. Scrape off the piled-up salt with a dull knife. Then rinse the supersalted side under the faucet with lukewarm water. (Cold water dissolves salt better, but it also chills the steak.) Finish the job by pouring any grease that's still in the broiler pan into a can, and wiping out the pan. You can do the big cleaning job later. Set the broiler rack down a couple of notches in the oven, and shove the whole thing back, washed side up, for a couple of minutes with the broiler turned on again. This sizzles it a little and puts it back in character. Somewhere along the line, if you have a kitchen exhaust fan, you should turn it on to pull the smoke out. But don't do it until you stop the big blaze.

If your blazing nightmare should, by any chance, be completely conquered without any of your prospective diners knowing about it, for heaven's sake don't tell them about it. They'll never know the difference. You've probably expounded on the glories of restaurant food that went through some well-concealed nightmare even worse.

THE RIGHT EXTINGUISHER

The easiest answer to the oven fire is the carbon dioxide fire extinguisher (CO_2). Just be *sure* it's a straight CO_2-type, nothing else. Essentially, this is a little tank of compressed gas of the same variety that makes the bubbles in your club soda. It has a trigger on it and usually some kind of a snout so you can aim it at the fire. Then when all hell breaks loose in your oven, you just shoot a quick blast of carbon dioxide at it and everything goes out. No nightmare, no salt, no lukewarm bath for the steak.

These wonderful little gas shooters aren't cheap (about the price of a good tire), but they're stout fellows. They can lick most car and boat fires along with burning wastebaskets in the house, and they'll usually save the day if you knock over your oil lamp during a power blackout.

REMEDIES FOR SCORCHED AND WARPED POTS AND PANS

Smoldering pots and pans, while not as spectacular, can also add a devilish touch to your kitchen activities. And if you do what comes naturally, you may make things worse. If you whisk the pot off the stove and squirt a stream of cold water into it, you may split the bottom—especially if the pot is a heavy one like a Dutch oven. Instead, set the pot aside for a minute or two on something fireproof, like an unused burner on the stove, or a plate. Then rinse it after it cools a little. Let your kitchen fan pull out the smell of your incinerated vegetables.

If the pan is Teflon-lined, mix half a cup of household bleach with a cup of water and two tablespoonfuls of baking soda, and boil the whole business in the pan to minimize or eliminate the heat stain. It's a good idea to use the kitchen fan while this is going on.

If the pan is aluminum, mix a solution of two tablespoonfuls of cream of tartar in a quart of water, and boil it in the pan for five or ten minutes. Then let it soak until things soften inside. You can use the same formula to clean your coffee pot better than you can with plain baking soda.

But whatever you do, don't get the Teflon and aluminum formulas mixed up. They're not interchangeable.

Roly-poly pots and pans that rock around wherever you put them are a lesser kitchen jangler. If the man of the house owns a plastic-headed hammer (often used on chisels) or a rubber fender mallet, he can turn the pot upside down (with some rags between it and the kitchen counter) and give it a good whack on the bottom. This flattens the bottom and stops the pot from rocking in the future. If you don't happen to have one of the fancy hammers just lay a block of wood or some paperback book you don't like on the bottom of the inverted pot and whack that with an ordinary hammer. In any event, try a moderate whack first. If that doesn't do the trick, use a harder whack. Just don't vent your spleen on it and squash the pot.

HOW TO SHARPEN A KNIFE

While knives don't rank as appliances, they're mighty important tools around the kitchen, and they're a real nuisance if they're not sharp. The best way to sharpen them these days is with an electric knife sharpener, if you're lucky enough to have one. But even then there's a trick to getting the best results. First, push the button that starts the sharpener. Then lower the handle end of the blade into the knife slot (some sharpeners also have a scissors slot) until it comes into contact with the grinding wheel or wheels *gently*. As soon as the blade touches the grinding element, draw the blade through the slot at an even speed and at a gentle and even pressure. Don't bear down enough to slow the grinder.

And be sure to tip the knife handle upward as the tip of the blade reaches the grinder, so you sharpen the curved end of the cutting edge. You use this part of the blade in much of your carving. The number of times you pass the blade through the sharpener depends on the dullness of the blade. If the edge is so badly dulled that it's actually visible as a rounded surface, keep at the job until you can see it's ground to a cutting edge. This may take half a dozen passes or more. People who know how test the sharpness by sliding a fingertip *across* the cutting edge. *Never*—repeat—*never* slide your finger along the blade lengthwise. A really keen blade can give you a serious cut this way before you even know it happened. If you want to play it safe (and why not?), try the blade on a piece of meat. That's what you'll use it on anyway. But wipe it with a sponge before you test it. This removes any minute metal or abrasive particles that may be on it.

Nonelectric sharpeners are made in several types. One familiar form consists of groups of little hardened metal disks arranged in two meshing rows. You simply slide the cutting edge of the knife blade along the groove where the rows of disks meet, drawing it toward you and tipping it at the end to sharpen the curved portion. These do a creditable job, too. You can test the sharpness as outlined earlier. But protect them from corrosion.

Carbide knife sharpeners, among the most modern nonelectric types, are often not much bigger than half a goose egg, and sometimes shaped something like an egg, too. The Aladdin, for example, made by the New England Carbide Tool Company, of Medford, Massachusetts, mounts on the wall or a door with a single screw. You simply draw the knife blade through the slot a few times, tilting, as with other types, and the job's done. The carbide sharpening cutters are made of the same material used in drills for boring concrete.

The steel is the old familiar aid to the chef and the man who carves the roast. It is simply a round, tapered steel shaft with fine ridges running lengthwise along it, and a handle at the large end. You use it to keep your knife sharp after the sharpener has done the big job. To understand how the steel works, it helps to know that the cutting edge of a fine knife actually appears saw-toothed under the microscope. The tiny teeth are created by the abrasive grains of the grinder, or by the abrasive action of metal sharpening cutters. As a knife dulls, these little teeth bend over to one side or the other. The steel straightens the good ones and shears off the weak ones, putting a new, keen edge on the blade. The correct technique for using the steel calls for sliding the blade of the knife lengthwise along the steel while sliding the cutting edge across the steel so its entire length rides over the steel's ridges. Chefs do it by sliding the knife toward them on the steel, first on top of it, then under it, so as to treat both sides of the cutting edge. The steel has a guard at the handle end to prevent the blade from striking the user's hand. Home carvers often prefer to slide the knife away from them on the steel in the same over-and-under manner. Either way, the blade of the knife should be tilted so the cutting edge meets the steel at about the same angle as that formed by the two surfaces of a match pack. You can't get very precise about this, as most fine knives are hand-ground at the factory and the angle of the actual cutting edge varies from one to another, even in the same brand. But they're all good and sharp. A tip: if you find the steel isn't restoring the sharpness to your knife, tilt the blade just a little more when you use the steel. When the steel no longer restores the keen edge, it's time for the sharpener again. But use the steel before each carving job to reduce the number of actual sharpenings required. The steel removes less metal from the blade and prolongs its useful life.

6

FURNITURE TROUBLES AND HOUSEHOLD SQUEAKS

WOBBLY CHAIRS and squeaky stairs are easier to fix than they used to be. Special nails and modern glues help a lot. They can help so much, in fact, that it will be worth your while to familiarize yourself with the important ones before you even think about tackling a wobble or squeak repair. The important glues are described in Chapter 14 along with their special qualities. Many of them can do things that glue could never do before. That's why they can take so much of the work out of many furniture repairs. As to the special nails, they're more limited in the amount of work they can save you, but today's spiral-fluted flooring nails, those extra-hard versions of the old familiar screw nail, can often enable you to kill a maddening squeak forever with just a few hammer whacks. You'll also find the details on using these nails in Chapter 14. Now for the tricks of the trade.

HOW TO FIX A WOBBLY CHAIR

Chairs wobble when legs are loose in the seat, or rungs are loose in the legs, or both. The longer you neglect it, the worse the wobble becomes. Each time the legs tilt, they bump the edges of the holes where they're supposed to fit snugly, and make the holes a little bigger. And the edges of the holes dig into the tenons on the tops of the legs and make matters worse. While this is going on, the rungs are doing much the same thing. Sooner or later the whole thing can skew far enough out of kilter to snap something. Then the whole business collapses, and you're on the floor. But most of us dread the repair job (if we even consider it) because it means pulling all those joints apart so everything can be recoated with glue and put back together again. One trouble is that part of the thing is usually still tight and won't come apart. So we place the chair carefully where we hope nobody will sit on it. But somebody always does—finally.

Thanks to modern glues (call them adhesives if you're technically minded), you can fix wobbly chairs without pulling them apart. The easiest ones to use are the white glues that come in squeeze bottles under a variety of trade names, (such as Elmer's Glue-All) and the newer aliphatic resin types like Titebond. Both are actually stronger than most furniture needs, and both may be thinned slightly with water. This is part of the trick of dribble gluing—which works very well, especially in the worst cases, and requires very little effort or intelligence.

To start, turn the wobbly chair upside down and wiggle all the parts that will wiggle, taking a good look at the joints to see how much they open up when you shove the parts one way or the other. If they open enough to slip in a little sliver of thin paper, that's enough. Now fill a jigger glass about half full of either of the glues mentioned in the preceding paragraph, and add a little water—just a few drops at a time, stirring it in with a toothpick or drink stirrer. You don't want the glue watery, but like very light cream, so it will be drawn into the loose spaces in the chair joints by capillary action.

Use a sliver of wood or a plastic spoon to dribble the glue all the way around each loose joint where the legs fit into the underside of the chair seat of solid-seat chairs. Do the same on all other types of joints where one part fits into a hole in the other. Wiggle the whole business around so the loose spaces in the joints will shift to let the glue in on all sides. You can help squish the glue in with your finger tip, too. From the true craftsman's point of view, this makes you strictly a nonconformist of a decidedly sloppy sort. But you will cure your wobbles. Use a wet rag or cellulose sponge to wipe off excess glue smeared around the chair joints. And leave the chair upside down overnight. If it has a tendency to slant or twist in a way it shouldn't, use some twine, tied diagonally from one part to another, to pull it back in shape while the glue is still fresh. Before you use the chair, look for open spaces still showing in the joints. If they're fairly large, dribble in a little more glue and, if necessary, shove in a little sliver of wood. You can whittle the sliver off of a scrap piece, even a twig. Then leave the thing to harden for another night.

If you've really worked the glue into the cracks, the finished job will be rock-solid. You don't have to worry if you happen to notice a glue trickle on the finish too late to wipe it off. When the glue is thoroughly dry, it probably won't show, anyway, as both glues dry practically transparent, and they don't stick well to finished surfaces. So, if need be, you can peel the glue off, dampening it for a while first, if it needs to be softened.

CURING A SHAKY TABLE

Table wobble is treated in much the same manner as chair troubles. Before you get out the glue bottle, however, it's a good idea to hold your finger against the cracks in the various joints while pushing the table to make it wobble. (This may call for a helper.) Your finger will tell you where the movement is. This is important in tables that have removable legs, in case you ever have to dismantle the parts for moving or storage. Use glue to lock the glued joints that are loose, but don't use it on joints that are intended to come apart. Almost always you'll be able to stiffen come-apart joints completely by tightening the screws or wing nuts that hold them.

TYPICAL PROBLEMS WITH CABINETS

Cabinets seldom appear to be wobbly, but they can fool you. If a cabinet door sticks, look around the edge of it for a scraped area that shows where it's rubbing against the frame in closing. Sometimes the scrape shows plainly on the frame without need for a close look.

If the door is sagging, the rub point will be at the lower corner on the latch side of the door. With the door partially opened, lift that side of it. If you feel an upward movement or play, take a look at the hinges. About half the time this type of trouble is caused simply by loose hinges. If this is it, just tighten the hinge screws, and your troubles are licked.

When the hinges are tight but there's still play in the door, you'll find looseness in the door itself. Usually this amounts to play between the central panel of the door and the frame. There are, however, numerous variations. But you can track down the source of trouble by the same finger-tip method mentioned for tables. Hold your finger against the joint or seam line between parts of the door as you lift its latch edge and release it. Wherever there's movement between parts (which there shouldn't be), you'll feel it. Cure it as previously outlined, by letting slightly thinned glue seep into the loose joints. But be sure to wipe off trickles on central panels of cabinet doors, as any remaining trace on such flat surfaces stands out much more than on chair and table legs.

The wiggly cabinet carcass

When hinges and door parts are tight and tidy but a corner still binds on the latch side of the door, the cabinet's skeleton is the culprit. It's twisted out of shape for one reason or another. Old furniture sometimes gets that way from repeated humid weather attacks over the years. Old-time animal glues, though stronger than wood, are weakened by moisture. And if uneven floors get into the picture, the cabinet skews to fit the floor.

If the door's latch edge rubs at the lower corner, try lifting the corner of the cabinet nearest the hinge side of the same door. If this stops the rubbing, simply push a wedge or shim under the leg at the corner to make the cure permanent. A few layers of cardboard usually make a good shim. Or you can use a scrap of floor tile, or a mustard paddle or tongue depressor. Think a little about how this corner lifting works, and you'll quickly see how hoisting the opposite corner can relieve doors that stick at the upper corners. Once the cabinet doors are working freely, you can dribble glue into the inside seams of the cabinet joints between sides, bottom, and back.

RIPPLED VENEER

Another of the traditional furniture headaches is the rippled veneer problem. It's likely to occur when you persist in leaving something damp standing on top of a veneered piece of furniture, like a table or desk. Flowerpots resting in saucers or plates during hot, humid weather, are typical troublemakers. The water from the flowerpot seeps down into the saucer, then evaporates, cooling the saucer just enough to sweat underneath. This traps moisture against the furniture finish, and can loosen the veneer over a period of time. The moisture also swells the veneer at the moist area so it tends to bulge upward. The same thing can result from a steady downflow of cold, moist air from a window—if the piece of furniture is directly under it.

The sooner you spot this type of trouble, the better. When the veneer separation is merely a loose, but near-flat blister, the repair job is easiest. Lay a piece of tough paper (a section cut from a strong grocery bag is good) over the loosened veneer area. Then with an electric iron (not a steam iron) set at medium heat, go over the area with firm pressure once or twice. You will be able to feel the veneer blister flatten down. On the final pass, follow directly behind the iron with a cold, flat-surfaced object like a piece of ceramic tile. The hot iron softens the glues usually used in veneering, and the cool tile chills them hard again, preventing the flattened area from reseparating. Try to do this job quickly to minimize heat damage to the finish. Some refinishing of the area is usually necessary, however.

LOCATING AND ELIMINATING SQUEAKS IN STAIRS AND FLOORS

When things like floors and stairs squeak, they do it because something moves and rubs against something else. It sometimes happens because the flooring or stair treads were installed during a long spell of very humid weather. After everything was nailed down tight, the wood shrank a little and the nail heads got some play under them. After that the wood began to ride up and down on the nails here and there with the weight of people walking. In other cases, everything was done properly in the first place but you left your house unheated and soggy damp while you languished on the beach in Florida during a vacation trip. The dampness swelled the wood in your house. Your flooring strips swelled against each other so hard they actually crushed their edge fibers, causing what the pros call flooring set. Then when you came back and turned on the heat, everything dried out and shriveled a little, leaving cracks in your floor and space under nail heads. So when you walk around your house now, you hear squeaks. You did the damage, of course. It's your own stupid fault. But you want to cure it. How do you do it? Let's take the floor first.

Rock, squeak, and listen

Floor squeaks can be deceptive. To pin down their location, get some willing soul to rock back and forth on the squeaky area while you put your ear close to the floor. Use your finger tip again, too, holding it across seams between suspected flooring strips. If you feel any movement, you are doubly sure of the squeak spot. But your ear alone should do the trick.

The cures depend on the house

Once you've tracked down your squeak, your corrective surgery depends on your house. If you have an old-time rugged cellar without princely paneling and bedazzled ceiling, you can do the job in sneaky fashion, leaving no scars, no traces.

You start by standing in the cellar while your friend rocks about overhead, squeaking the squeak for you. You can hold your hand against the underside of the subfloor above and actually feel the squeak if it's a good one. Then you bore a little hole up into the very heart of the noisy area to take a wood screw that will pull everything tight. The total thickness of your subfloor and finish floor is a little less than an inch and a half if the subfloor is tongue-and-groove sheathing boards. If the subfloor is plywood, there's some variation, so measure the thickness where it shows at cellar stairs or any other opening. Then use a drill bit, like a Screwmate, that drills the hole for the threaded part of the screw, the smooth shank, and the countersunk (flat) head all in one shot. You can do the job with a crank-handled hand drill or an electric drill—if you happen to have received one for your birthday or Christmas. Just be sure the drill bit you use is just a little too short to come all the way through. Your best bet: buy your screws and your drill bits at the same hardware store at the same time—so they'll match. The bits are usually sold in sets of three or four, mounted on a card. Each time you drive a screw up into the floor, yell for your helper to do some more rocking. As soon as the squeak stops, you can quit. It may take three or four screws to

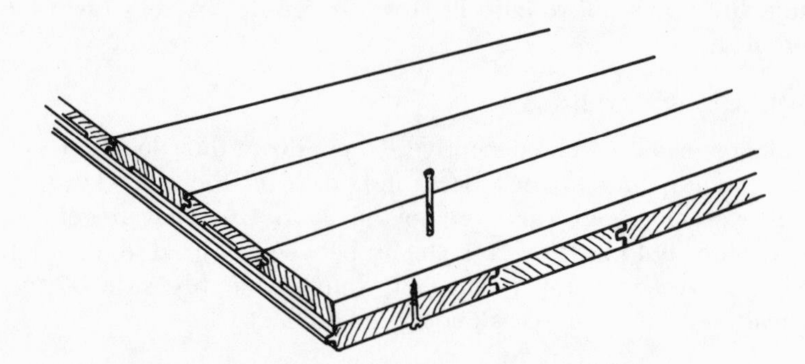

If you drive a screw from below (if the basement is unfinished), make sure it doesn't come all the way through the finished floor above. It should end just short of the upper surface, as shown. If the basement is finished with a ceiling that prevents driving the screw from below, use a spiral-fluted screw type flooring nail, driven down from above. If it sticks through the subflooring, it doesn't matter, as it's concealed by the basement ceiling.

complete the silencing. It's important to get the screws good and tight. A bit brace (that big, hand-crank tool for boring holes) with a screwdriver bit does the job with the least effort. If you don't have one of these things and don't feel like buying one, use an offset screwdriver. This is a little crank-handle screwdriver that fits in the palm of your hand—but it provides plenty of leverage. You can find one at most hardware stores for less than a dollar.

If you have a fancy basement

If your basement is finished off to the Queen's taste as a recreation room with a beautiful ceiling that prevents you from reaching the underside of the floor without committing mayhem, there's still an easy answer. Go down to your hardware store or lumberyard and ask to see some spiral-fluted flooring nails. These look as if they started out as square, heavy wire and then were twisted in candy-stripe fashion. As they're made under several trade names, you may have to explain this to the hardware clerk—though lumber dealers know what you're looking for without much ado.

The spiral nails can be driven down through the flooring strips, and have much greater holding power than conventional nails. To avoid splitting the flooring, drill pilot holes for the nails about 25 per cent smaller than the smooth-shank portion of the nails. It's a good idea, too, to drill a shallow hole of sufficient diameter to take the nail head, so it can be recessed and filled over with Plastic Wood, Wood Dough, or a similar compound. As with screws from underneath, use as many spiral nails as required to silence the squeak.

On stairs

In days gone by, when the underside of a stairway was often exposed as the ceiling of another stairway (the cellar stairs were often under the grand front stairs), you could usually stop stair squeaks by tapping the stair wedges tighter. These were plainly visible wooden wedges under the treads of the stairs. Today you usually can't reach the underside of the stairs, and quite a few stairways are machine-made without the wedges anyway. So you work from the top. Yell for your helper to start the action, as in floor-squeak pursuit, and have him rock his weight on the squeaky stair tread while your fingertip feels along the seams for movement. It's likely to be along the front edge of the tread (step) as air circulation above the step makes the upper surface a little drier than the confined undersurface, and tends to make the wood cup slightly concave on top occasionally. The cure depends on the patient.

If there's so much movement that filler has been pushed out above the heads of the nails that hold the steps to the stringers (the side members into which the steps are notched), you can probably stop the squeak by driving a few spiral flooring nails between the loose nails. But drill pilot holes.

WHEN YOU CAN'T USE A HAMMER

If experience has shown you that hammering on parts of your particular house has a way of causing plaster cracks or other I-wish-I-hadn't-tried-it headaches, there's a cabinetmaker's tool that may save the day. It's usually called a glue injector and you'll find it at cabinetmaker's supply houses like Albert Constantine and Son, of New York. Basically, it resembles an overgrown hypodermic syringe with a snout that shoots glue through a drilled hole into joints and gaps. Drill a snout-sized hole where you would otherwise drive a nail, and shoot in a dose of gap-filling glue like casein glue (Casco) or aliphatic glue (Titebond). Don't thin the glue any more than necessary to allow it to pass through the injector, and clean the injector immediately afterward. You can often use the same gadget on floors and loose furniture joints that can't be fixed any other way.

HOW TO REPLACE LOST CARVINGS

If the railing, newel post, or balusters of your stairs are lacking some of their artistic swirls through the activities of some vile previous owner of the house, or through the normal pursuits of your children, you may be surprised at the easy solutions that are possible. Unless your house is a very old one, for example, you can probably match everything from newel post to balusters at your nearest lumberyard. If the missing ornamentation is older and more elaborate, small details can be molded from Plastic Wood or Wood Dough and finished to match the original—but allow two days' drying time before painting. You want to be sure the plastic solvent won't lift the paint.

Replacing the royal touch

If you are the proud owner of an old mansion done in the grand tradition, and half the great coat of arms is missing from the mantelpiece, and some historic heraldic masterpiece has chunked away from the arch of the great entrance hall, you have two chances to restore the glories of old. And the same two chances will probably bring back the original splendor to the battered old sideboard you blundered into collecting at the antique auction.

If the missing art work is of moderate size like a parade of lions and unicorns with grand dukes rampant across a fireplace front, you may be startled to find a perfect replacement in the cabinet-maker's supply catalogue. If only a part of some such magnificent bas relief is missing, you're still likely to save trouble by replacing the whole business with the nearest approximation of the design. If the missing part is just a small tip at one end, tape a piece of paper over the same section of the other end and look at the result from a few feet away. Maybe the easiest answer, if it doesn't look peculiar, is simply the removal of the papered-over section to make things balance up.

For big parts, try the house wrecker

If something big is missing, like a rotted-out chunk of a post on your Victorian front porch, start shopping around the house wreckers' storage yards. You'll never be the same but you'll have a lot of fun, and you'll probably save money after you get over your first buying spree.

The bargain wonderland of the house wrecker results from the fact that a major portion of his income is derived from selling things and materials salvaged from wrecked buildings and houses. All kinds of lumber sell for just half the price of new lumber in most cases. You can buy lathe-turned colonial columns, gargoyles, chandeliers, furniture, doors, windows, weather vanes, sometimes even pigs, pigeons, antique automobiles, and cabin cruisers. The reason: most demolition contracts give the wrecker title to everything on the premises when the wrecking job begins, even the shrubbery. The prices for odd-ball items depend largely on the demand, and range from around a nickel upward—sometimes giving even the wrecker a dizzy feeling. The doorknobs from New York's old Ritz-Carlton Hotel, for example, sold by the thousands at $25 apiece. And people were still eager for more years later. Yet, at the same time, you could buy a complete used elevator for $75—only the price of three doorknobs.

If you're looking for parts to fit a city house, go to a city wrecker. If you're restoring a country house, go to a country wrecker. The same general rule applies to furniture. But try to keep your mind on your business. Even the small wrecker usually has more than one million separate items for sale at bargain rates. And some of the things may tend to distract you. One New England wrecker who demolished a carnival warehouse, for example, recently sold a stuffed calf with two heads for less than $3. Items like this, though they may not conform precisely to your present decorative theme, may nevertheless find a place in your planning.

GENERAL TIPS

If whatever you're trying to fix, from a box to a banister, is made of wood, you'll do well to keep a few simple rules in mind. First, if you have to drive a nail or a screw near the end or the edge of a wooden part, drill a pilot hole first to avoid splitting. And when you drive a nail into a finished surface, stop banging while the nail head is still a little above the surface. Then hold a nail set against the head of the nail and drive it the rest of the way by hammering on the other end of the nail set. The nail set is just a piece of metal rod with a flat head on one end (for hammering) and a tip tapered to nail diameter on the other (to seat on the nail head). It's usually just about the cheapest tool you can buy, so you should have one.

7

FIRST AID FOR NATURAL WOOD AND MARBLE FINISHES

MOST HOUSES are full of things finished to show the natural grain of the wood, plain or stained. These include your floors, stairs, stair rails, furniture, often even the interior trim. And when some clodhead messes up one of these finishes, it's a lot trickier to fix than a painted one. So the pages that follow provide you with the detailed remedies for some of the worst messes you're likely to encounter.

REMOVING RINGS

Rings from drinking glasses are probably the commonest wood-finish nuisance. The cure depends on the type of finish to some extent. If you know it's shellac, you can often cure the ring by dipping a little piece of lintless cloth in a jigger of clear shellac diluted five to one with denatured alcohol, and wiping it lightly around the ring. Don't overdo it. If it doesn't work quickly, quit and let everything dry.

Another method that works on many finishes is the pumice-and-oil or rottenstone-and-oil rubdown. If the ring is slight, use rottenstone and number 10 engine oil mixed to a creamy paste. If it's a big, bleary ring, use pumice instead of rottenstone because it cuts a little faster. If you don't have any engine oil around, you can use vegetable cooking oil. Make a little pad of lint-free cloth, plop it into the paste, and rub it over the ring area, not just around the ring. This usually gets rid of the ring in short order. But wipe the area clean at *very* short intervals as you work, and stop rubbing as soon as the job's done. Otherwise you may rub through the finish. In any event, if the original surface is one of the superglossy ones common today, the repaired area will end up with a softer luster. This is a very attractive finish in itself, and a practical one because slight blemishes don't stand out like bullet holes. So you may decide you'd like to soften the luster of the entire surface. If so, just give the whole thing a light rubdown with rottenstone and oil. For the big job, you can thin out the paste with a little more oil for easier large-area working. And again, don't overdo it. If you want to increase the gloss of the repaired area to match the original gloss (instead of softening the over-all finish), use a hard wax like Simoniz, and buff it thoroughly. You can hand-buff with a soft cloth and elbow grease. But if you have a power drill (described in Chapter 2), you can do a terrific job with almost no effort by using the drill with a buffing bonnet slipped over its rubber sanding disk. Before you begin any waxing, however, clean off the surface with a big rag well moistened with turpentine, then wipe dry. Simonizing furniture, incidentally, greatly increases the resistance of the finish to ring formation.

DEEP AND SHALLOW SCRATCHES

Scratches usually appear much lighter than the area around them because of light refracted by the broken particles of transparent finish. So the first step in the scratch-cure is brushing all loose particles from the scratch. Then if you know what the original finishing material was, you can trail a tiny line of it into the scratch, using a toothpick or a pin, depending on the scratch size. When it's dry, blend it out with very fine sandpaper pulled over your finger tip and worked very lightly in a circular motion (about ½ inch circles) along the scratch. Then wax it. Very tiny scratches often disappear with waxing alone. If you try the wax first, however, and it doesn't quite do the trick, wipe out the waxed scratch with turpentine before you try the other method.

If a scratch goes so deep it exposes raw, unstained wood, you can either touch it up with a matching wood stain (mahogany, walnut, etc.) or use what you happen to have on hand. Brown shoe polish does a creditable job on the usual mahogany, especially if the polish is slightly on the reddish side. Black ink is generally good on dark walnut and similar finishes. Kitchen Bouquet (for coloring gravy) does very well on maple and antique pine finishes, as on Early American pieces. And you can dilute it to get a close match. After you use one of these pinch hitters, however, apply some kind of finish over it to lock it in. Toothpicks and pipe cleaners make good applicators for the makeshift stains and the finishes, too.

HOW TO USE FILLERS FOR DIGS AND DENTS

Digs and dents call for a different technique because they are too big to fill in with finish alone. If the dig is in a broad, flat surface where it really shows, the best stuff to fill it with is stick shellac or stick lacquer. The method is the same, but always read the directions, as you may find you have some new type with a gimmick to it. To do it right, you need a thin, flexible metal spatula (like the kitchen variety), an old table knife you don't care about, and an alcohol lamp or a propane torch. You can buy the alcohol lamp in a big drugstore if you don't own a propane torch. Even the kitchen range may do if it's close to the repair job. The object of all this is simply a source of fairly high heat that doesn't also make soot.

You select the stick shellac in a color that matches the dented finish as closely as possible. (The sticks are usually about the size of French fried potatoes, around 2½ inches long, and they don't cost much.) Big paint stores stock them. If you're not sure of your color judgment, buy two or three that seem about right but vary a little.

Hold the tip of the old table knife in the flame and push the end of the shellac stick against it while still in the flame to soften it. Do this close to the dent so you can dribble the shellac into the dent without spilling elsewhere, as soon as the heat makes it runny enough. Don't get it so hot that it smokes, or it'll scorch and foul up. As soon as the dent is slightly over-filled, smooth it off with the spatula. As the spatula should be hot for the job, it's a good idea to have a helper, so you don't need four hands of your own. The well-warmed spatula also serves to skim off any excess filler that happens to smear beyond the dented area. You can finish off the job after it's hard with a rottenstone rubdown and a waxing.

If the dig is in the edge of a table top or if it resulted in a piece of carving being chipped off of something, one of the mushy fillers like Plastic Wood or Wood Dough will usually be handier than stick shellac for the repair. Buy a small can of the filler in a light or dark tone to match the job. Use a little piece of sandpaper to roughen the surface it must stick to. Then push it in and smooth it off with a knife or spatula. It's soft as it comes. You don't have to heat it. But wipe off any that gets on the surrounding surface, as the solvent in it will mar the finish.

If you have to duplicate a small, chipped-off piece of carving, this kind of filler is easy to shape with your fingers. Let it harden overnight. After that you can sand it, even trim-shape it with a sharp knife. And if it has shrunk a little in drying, you can add to it. If you want to apply a wood finish over it, let it dry for an extra day or two to eliminate all the solvent. Once hard, you can treat it like wood—drill it, saw it, and so forth.

REMOVING CIGARETTE BURNS

Cigarette burns in table tops are seldom discovered until the party's over. As a first step in the repair, many furniture lovers feel you should locate the person who did the damage and belt him in the mouth. Otherwise you can begin by brushing the scorched area clean. Then cut an inch-wide strip from a standard sheet of 80-grit open-coat aluminum oxide abrasive paper. This may sound like a mouthful but you can buy it in most any hardware store. The 80-grit is one of the medium grades of coarseness. The "open coat" means that the abrasive grains are scattered farther apart on the paper than usual, so they won't clog as quickly with the charred-finish particles. And the "aluminum oxide" refers to one of the fastest-working of all abrasives.

Pull the strip of abrasive paper business-side out, over the tip of your right-hand index finger, and start rubbing it with gentle pressure and circular motion along the charred area. Blow away the char dust as you work. Stop about every five seconds (yes, really) and slap the char out of the paper, or shift to a clean part of the paper strip. This keeps the char from being ground into the clean wood when you reach it. As you work, blend your sanding out beyond the limits of the charred area, feathering out onto the finish around it. On dark-finished tables you don't have to carry the sanding as far as on light ones, as some trace of char will be concealed by the touch-up stain that comes afterward. On blond pieces, however, the black has to go completely. Once you've sanded away the charcoal, you simply refinish the area. If it's stained, you'll usually have to touch up areas that have been sanded to a lighter tone. You can do this with matching stain on a dime-store artist's brush. Or, for better control, wet a small cloth pad with the stain, then squeeze out most of it. Then rub the too-light areas with the squeezed-out cloth. Repeat the process, adding a little stain to the cloth if necessary, until you get the right tone. This way you avoid the risk of getting it too dark in one shot. Either way, let the stain dry thoroughly before you apply the wood finish that restores the luster.

REMOVING DYE STAINS

Some of the things you may use in drinks, from colorful cherries to other things that come in very small bottles to provide the master's touch, can penetrate many finishes very quickly with kaleidoscopic results, especially on light-toned finishes. If this happens, you have to make a tough decision: do nothing, and learn to live with the bloody-looking mess, or try to fix it and maybe make matters worse.

If you decide to gamble on a repair, do it as quickly as possible while the stain is still fresh. Mix a little household bleach half-and-half with water, soak a rag with it, and mop it over the stain. In many cases this works like magic, and the stain vanishes while you watch. If it doesn't work that fast, dry the area with another rag quickly and examine the surface for any signs that the finish is being damaged—signs like little wrinkles or cracks. If all's well, you can continue the treatment. And keep watching the stain for signs that it's fading. Often the stain fades out gradually. Whatever happens, slosh off the area when you're through, using plenty of clear water.

OVER-ALL REFINISHING

Very few cases of severe damage to finely finished wood can be concealed completely by easy repair methods. But lots of them can be hidden so well nobody but you is likely to notice them. In some instances, refinishing the entire surface may do the trick when touch-up methods won't. This is often true when your touch-up leaves wide variations in luster. If this is your worry, just sand the whole business lightly with very fine sandpaper (called cabinet paper), dust it off thoroughly, and apply another coat of finish over the whole business. When this is thoroughly hard, rub it down lightly with rottenstone and oil. This not only gives it an even, attractively soft luster, but it removes the tiny dust particles that stick out like sore thumbs on a high gloss. If you want a perfect, dust-free high-gloss finish, you can either build yourself a dust-free spray booth about as big as a small living room, or send the job out to be done professionally.

As to the types of finishes to use on major jobs, just be sure the one you're going to use won't act like paint remover on the one it's going on top of. This is more of a problem in this era of superchemistry. If you're in doubt, shellac or plain old spar varnish are friendly to most finishes. And spar varnish formulated for outdoor use isn't likely to develop rings from highball glasses.

Over bare wood, as on unfinished furniture or after complete paint removal, shellac has an interesting advantage. You can wipe it on a coat at a time (after thinning, as instructed on the can) so you never get brush marks. Use a lintless cloth pad. It takes quite a few wiped-on coats, but, topped off with hard wax, it's a beautiful finish. Many of the warm furniture tones are possible simply by mixing clear and orange shellac in the proportion that gives the result you want. You can prestain the wood, of course. And if you find the effect isn't quite what you expected, you can add color to the shellac itself, with dyes made for the purpose.

A good idea if you have a magnificent piece of furniture that really needs major refinishing: Buy a cheap piece of junk-shop furniture with the same kind of finish (mahogany, blond, walnut, etc.) and try the methods described—on different parts of it. Then use the one you like best.

REPAIRING RAVAGED MARBLE

Often used with natural-finished wood, marble is another material that often loses its beauty through the ravages of careless people. Handsome marble furniture tops frequently end their careers cracked and broken, dulled and stained. Yet anyone can restore the original beauty to even a shattered, scratched, dulled, and stained piece. All it takes is the right materials, some elbow grease (if you have no power drill), and a reasonable amount of patience. As stains are the commonest ailments, we'll tackle those first.

Rust stains, often found on carelessly stored antiques, may be a blessing in disguise, as they frequently result in a lower selling price. If you think the stain may be a recent one, try energetic rubbing with a piece of hard (not soft) cloth. If the stain hasn't penetrated deeply, this often takes it off. If the stain has gone deeper, it calls for a trip to the drugstore. You need a small amount of sodium hydrosulfite crystals and a little sodium citrate solution. Sprinkle the sodium hydrosulfite crystals over the stained area, moisten them with water, and let the whole business stand for no more than half an hour. Then rinse it all off with water and wet down the area with the sodium citrate solution. If the first try at this procedure leaves some of the stain still showing, do it again. When all's well, rinse everything off. With this treatment the usual rust stain fades out while you're watching it. If the stain is very deep and the job has to be repeated, a little surface etching may result. You can smooth this up by repolishing the area as described later.

Tobacco and plant leaf stains can be removed easily with hydrogen peroxide of hair-bleach strength. If the stain is a husky one, you can keep the peroxide from evaporating, so as to prolong its effect, by mixing it to a paste with talcum powder and spreading it over the stain. To get the stain-removing reaction going, you add a few drops of household ammonia. When the mix stops bubbling, wash it all off with water. You can use the talcum powder-paste trick also for the purpose of making the solution stick to a vertical surface, like a fireplace front.

Ink stains. First rinse these stains with clear water. Then drench two pieces of blotting paper—one with household ammonia, the other with denatured alcohol. Apply them to the stain alternately, a few minutes at a time. If a stain remains from a metallic ink, it can be eliminated by the same procedure used on rust.

Iodine stains, such as you may get on a marble counter around your bathroom washbasin, are no great problem. Just mix a paste of denatured alcohol and talcum powder and spread it over the stain. One treatment usually does it if you catch the stain early.

Grease stains come off fast by merely rubbing them with a soft cloth soaked in acetone or mineral spirits. If they're heavy, puddle a little of the liquid on the stains for a few minutes, then mop it off.

Paint. Scrape dried paint off with a single-edge razor blade or a razor blade scraper made for removing paint from window panes. Use ordinary paint remover to remove any absorbed paint. If some color persists, bleach it with peroxide. Acetone will take care of the oil blotch that sometimes remains.

If you have a lot of marble around your house and you don't enjoy fiddling with chemicals, you can buy a kit of stain removers all ready to use from the Vermont Marble Company, of Proctor, Vermont. Then, when you spot a stain, all you have to do is open the right bottle.

Dulled marble. It's much easier than you think to polish a drab old piece of marble to such a glasslike sparkle you can see your face in it. You can do it by hand if you have no power tools, but, of course, it takes a lot less effort if you happen to have a little power drill and a sanding attachment.

Whether you work by hand or power, you start with 80-grit abrasive (if the marble is really worn completely dull), and progress through 120, 220, and 320. You can buy all of these at your hardware store in sheet abrasive paper form. You can also get them in the form of abrasive blocks from marble suppliers like the one mentioned earlier. If you use the sheet form, wrap it around a wood block for hand sanding. In power sanding don't use a flexible rubber disk sander (the usual type), as it has a tendency to leave semicircular scratches. Instead, use a ball-jointed rigid disk type like the Stanley Swirlaway. This seats flat on the marble surface even though the power drill is occasionally tilted somewhat. Whatever the sanding method, use each abrasive grade to remove roughness and scratches of a coarseness comparable to its grit. In other words, use the coarsest grade to remove all visible scratches. Then use successive grades to smooth the texture left by preceding grades.

The 320-grit abrasive will produce a fine satiny finish. Follow this with very fine sanding with 500-grit abrasive paper. If your hardware store doesn't have this, you can get it from auto body finish suppliers. If you buy the wet-or-dry type, you can rinse the surface while you're working. This reduces abrasive clogging and speeds the job. Also, when the surface is wet, you can get a good idea of what the final finish will be like. Let the surface dry (it takes only a few minutes) occasionally so you can check it for remaining scratches.

When you've done the abrasive smoothing and eliminated all noticeable scratches, you're ready for the final polishing. You do this with tin oxide powder available from marble suppliers like Vermont Marble. Mix it with water to make a creamy paste and spread it over the marble surface. If you have no power tools, you can rub the paste by hand with a felt or flannel pad. If you have a power drill and can get an orbital or reciprocal sanding attachment for it, use flannel in place of sandpaper. A power sander of either of the types will do as well as the drill attachment. (You can also use a rotating sanding attachment like the Swirlaway, but it will sling away the paste faster.) If the paste dries to a powder while you're working, add more water from time to time to keep it creamy. To tell when you have the desired degree of polish, wipe the marble clean occasionally and let it dry. You may have to wipe it several times with a moist cloth to remove the fine powder film that makes it look dull. Once you have the polish, you can expect it to last for years. If the marble happens to have any very deep scratches or chips, you don't have to sand and polish it all the way down to their depth to eliminate them. You can fill them with the marble glue described shortly. You make it match the marble with powdered pigments. The repair is then polished along with the rest of the marble surface.

Repairing broken marble is a surprisingly simple job when you use an adhesive made for the purpose, like Vermont Marble's Marfix (see page 162). First, fit all the broken parts together dry so you can see the correct position of the parts. You can also spot any holes where small pieces or chips are missing. You can fill these holes with a mixture of the glue and the correct pigment for the type of marble. You buy the pigment from the same company that supplies the glue you use.

Before you tackle the gluing job, mix a small test sample of the glue exactly according to the directions on the container. Keep poking at the surface of this sample with a stick or prod, and time its hardening with your watch. It's extremely important that you know how long it takes to harden. Otherwise you may not have time to get the pieces together after coating the broken edges with the glue. Reason for the test sample: the directions on the container are not always strictly accurate as to hardening time—and the room temperature may also affect it.

When you get ready for the final gluing job, be sure you have a perfectly *flat* surface to lay the marble on. Three-quarter-inch plywood is usually good enough. Whatever the supporting surface, cover it with at least two layers of newspaper to prevent the marble from sticking to the surface. Assemble the pieces dry, then slide them about an inch and a half apart so you can coat *both* edges of all meeting parts with the glue. Then slide the pieces together firmly, and skim off the squeezed-out glue with a putty knife or spatula. If there are chips along any of the glued seams, dribble extra glue into them to over-fill them slightly. When all pieces are together and the glue has dried, sand off all excess glue with 80-grit abrasive until the glue surface is just slightly higher than the marble surface. Then finish it off flush with successively finer grades. Use these grades also to repolish any marble areas roughened by the earlier step. When the broken parts fit together neatly without sizeable chips or gaps, very little after-polishing is necessary. The completed repair job conceals the breaks so well in most types of marble that a close examination is required to detect the fact that the piece was ever broken. This is especially true of marble with any figuring in it, as the natural color lines of the marble resemble the glue lines.

In using the marble glue, however, use caution in handling both the glue and the catalyst that makes it harden. The catalyst in most types is highly flammable and very dangerous to the eyes. When the glue hardens, however, it's as fire-safe as the adhesive used in fiberglass boats—roughly about the same as plywood.

8

PAPERING AND INTERIOR PAINTING

Unless your house is a dilapidated wreck, you should find interior painting or wallpapering a cinch. For some reason, however, people are forever telling grim tales about the preparation of cracked and crumbling walls or ceilings. Actually, the usual preparation, even including the repair of a few typical cracks, shouldn't take more than an hour or so. But you may have to let everything dry overnight before the actual refurbishing begins. This is especially true if cracks are involved.

PREPARING WALLS AND CEILINGS

About all the preparation you need bother with for most rooms is a dusting wipe with a soft cloth to get rid of dust and unnoticed cobwebs that may be hiding here and there. In kitchens and rooms near the kitchen, however, there's likely to be an oil film on the walls from cooking vapor, so you'll need to wash whatever you intend to paint. Carbona Wall-Wipe, used according to directions, lets you breeze through this phase of the job. Just be sure that you do your wall washing from the bottom up, not from the top down. You may think you're doing things backwards this way, but it works much better, as dirt doesn't pile on top of dirt, and you avoid streaks.

TREATMENT OF CRACKS

Whether your walls and ceilings are made of plaster or wallboard (gypsum board or sheetrock), the treatment of cracks is the same. The simplest repair material to use is Spackle. This is a white powder that looks like flour. You can buy it in assorted size boxes at hardware and paint stores. All you do to get it ready for use is mix it with water according to the directions on the box, though you'll probably end up mixing it with a free-hand touch. For small cracks it works nicely when it has about the consistency of soft toothpaste. Smear it into the cracks with a putty knife or even your finger tip, then smooth it off with the putty knife or a squeegee. In any event, the smoother you get the job while it's wet, the less sanding you'll need to do after it hardens. But it's nice to know you can sand any bumps smooth even when the stuff is hard. You'll probably like Spackle because it has a friendly way about it. If you have to sand off any bumps, use fine cabinet paper.

If any parts of your walls or ceilings are sagged and crumbling, don't fuss around trying to make your own repairs. When things are that much of a mess it's time to call in a professional to fix things up. Otherwise you may get your beautiful decorating all done when somebody slams a door and the whole ceiling lands on the floor. This kind of thing is very rare, but, as mentioned earlier, people are always talking about it.

REMOVING OLD STAINS

If there are any really bad stains on the wall or ceiling, particularly if they have a greasy or dye-type origin, take care of them before you start painting or papering. Some stains can even work their way through wallpaper. After you've removed as much of the stain as you can with something like Wall-Wipe (Soilax is another), play safe by sealing whatever blemish remains. Shellac is the long-standing favorite for sealing jobs, and it deserves its popularity. If you have time to allow about four hours between coats (more time than usually needed, but beneficial), use a couple of coats. After this, if you're going to paint the wall, there's a very important extra step. Mix some Spackle to medium cream consistency and *brush* it over the shellacked area like paint. Then let it dry before you apply your paint. The reason: the shellac sealing coat leaves the wall in that area shinier than the rest of the wall, and you'll see a very noticeable difference in finish with many paints. The Spackle coat brings the sealed area back to normal, so no blotch shows.

PAINTING METHODS

How to paint a wall

The paint roller takes most of the work out of the actual paint job and gets it done faster than ever was possible with a brush. But you still need a brush for cutting in. The cutting in consists of painting with a brush in all areas where the roller can't fit, or where it would bump against something. For example, you should brush-paint the strip of wall that directly adjoins the ceiling. Otherwise the end of your roller or some other part of it may smear paint on the ceiling. You do the same thing in corners and around door trim and around windows. The best way to arrange your schedule is to do the cutting in first. But do just a wall at a time, and follow up with the roller before you go to the next wall. By all means (unless you have a definite reason not to), use a water-mixed paint. It makes it a breeze to clean brushes and rollers, and it makes it much easier to get up spilled dribbles of paint.

Protecting the room's contents

If you're ambitious you can move everything out of the room—if you have any place to put it. But it's much easier to simply cover it right where it is. It helps if you shove movable things toward the center of the room. You can use old newspapers or polyethylene sheeting for protection. The polyethylene (something like heavy cellophane but chemically different) makes a wonderful dropcloth. It's cheap and waterproof, and it's easy to bundle away when you're through with it.

How to use a roller

First, don't fill the roller tray so full of paint that you can't get the roller into it without slopping paint overboard. Roll the roller down the tray's slope into the paint gently, then roll it back up again to distribute the paint all the way around the roller. Take a good look at this as you do it, and work out your own method of getting the paint all the way around. All this isn't vital, but it makes the painting go faster. Don't bear down so hard on the roller (as you roll it up the tray slope) that you squeeze all the paint out of it. But don't take it out of the tray splashing, soaked, and dripping. Moderation is the trick here—to avoid getting paint all over the place. One of the handiest things you can have is a cardboard from a laundered shirt—the kind the laundry puts in. Hold this under the roller as you carry it from the tray to the wall. And, by all means, hold it *under* the roller if you're painting a ceiling. It keeps you from having a varicolored mop of hair and a varicolored face.

When you set the freshly loaded roller against wall or ceiling, *don't* press hard on it. Roll it along with almost no pressure. Use just enough pressure to make it roll instead of slide. You'll get the hang of it in the first minute or two. Then as the paint is transferred to the wall, you can gradually press a little harder to wring out some more paint until you begin to notice skipped spots. Then it's time to reload the roller. There are all sorts of rules as to which way you should steer the roller around on the wall. The main thing is to get an even coating. Don't try to go too far on one roller loading. And don't get all upset because everything looks terrible at this stage. Some paints look as though you had tossed a tub of dishwater at the wall—until they dry. Then they look beautiful. Also, don't go back over areas that look thin—until they're dry. Modern interior paints often look thin while they're wet. If an area still looks thin after it's dry, go over it again.

Cleaning up afterward

As soon as the job is done, wash all your tools—brushes, rollers, everything. With water-mixed paint, plain cold water does the cleaning easily until the paint dries. After that it depends on the paint. Some are tough to get off. All this also applies to spilled blotches of paint on floors or furniture. If you have to go to the Grand Ball as soon as you finish painting, toss everything in a bucket of water to keep it from hardening until you get back. It helps to slosh it all around a little and maybe dump out the first water so everything can soak in fresh water.

WALLPAPERING

Wallpapering is preceded by the same kind of preparation as for painting. If there's already wallpaper on the walls, and if the old paper is firmly in place, you can put your new paper right over it. If the old paper seams were overlapped (you can tell by looking at them), it's a good idea to plan your papering job so the new seams come between the old ones—if possible. The idea here is that one seam on top of another is likely to be more conspicuous. But don't shake yourself to pieces worrying about it. It can look pretty good either way.

HOW MUCH PAPER TO GET

The first real step in the papering job is buying the right amount of paper. Instead of sweating over this, simply measure the perimeter of the room and the height of the ceiling. Then measure the dimensions of doorways and windows. Take these measurements to your wallpaper dealer and let him figure out how much you need. You should always buy at least one extra roll—but make an arrangement so you can take back any unused rolls. You'll do well to hang on to one unused roll, however, just in case some permissively trained brat (yours or your neighbor's) decides to scribble some pop art on your newly papered wall. This can be worse a couple of years later when the wallpaper design is no longer available.

MAKING NEAT SEAMS

Not too long ago the usual nonprofessional wallpapering job was done with overlapped seams. This resulted from the fact that wallpaper was usually sold with selvages on both edges like fabric. If you tried trimming these yourself, you were likely to get the edges too uneven for butting edge to edge. Now, however, most paper is sold pretrimmed, and when it isn't the dealer can trim it for you on a machine that does it just as well. So you might as well butt the seams edge to edge. This way there's no bump, however slight. Talk to your wallpaper dealer about this when you buy your paper. He'll make sure you get your paper in proper shape.

MATCHING PATTERNS

One reason why your wallpaper dealer will sell you more paper than you think you need is the fact that you have to match the wallpaper pattern from strip to strip. This means you'll have to shift strips up and down so the half of a rosebush on one strip fits exactly with the other half on the next strip. This is easy to do, but it means you'll occasionally waste some paper at the top or bottom of a strip. The best way to avoid trouble is to use your head a little right at the start. Decide how you want the pattern to be on the wall and cut the first strip accordingly. Then cut the rest of the strips for that wall, rolling out each one so as to match the pattern parts. And when you get ready to put the paper on the wall, make sure you have it right side up. Many a first wallpaper job has had the upside-down touch. Fortunately, most wallpapers look almost as pretty inverted.

THE EASY WAY TO APPLY PASTE

The chances are you don't own a table long enough to permit spreading wallpaper paste over a complete floor-to-ceiling strip in one step. But there's a trick that lets you do the job on a much shorter table. Before we get to that, however, there's an important point about the paste, itself. Don't let anybody talk you into making your own flour-and-water paste. The paste is the cheapest part of the job, anyway, and ready-made cellulose paste has lots of advantages. (Don't get this mixed up with cellulose nitrate cement—they're vastly different.)

To keep from smearing up the top of whatever table you use, you can cover it with some free corrugated cardboard. One side of a mattress or bicycle carton from one of your local stores will do the trick nicely. The paste is a simple water mix. To spread it on the paper, lay the paper (cut to a wall-height strip) back side up on the cardboard-covered table, with one end hanging over one end of the table. Then coat the area of the paper that is on

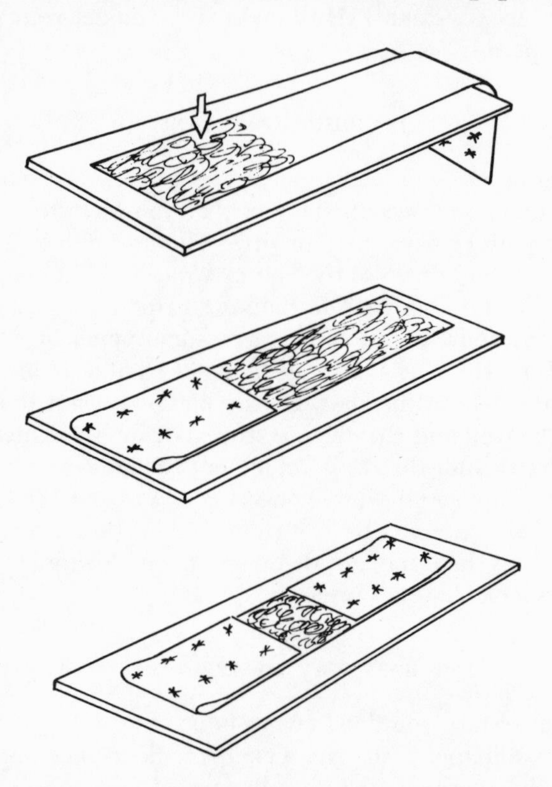

the table, and fold over the end as shown in the first drawing. Then you can slide the hanging-over end up onto the table and brush the paste on that. Then you can fold this end over as shown in the second drawing. *Do not* crease the ends where the paper is folded over. Leave it rounded, as shown. (The drawing is somewhat exaggerated.) This paste-to-paste fold-over makes it easy to carry the paper from the pasting table to the wall. If you don't have far to go, you can get along by folding over only one end. If you have to take the paper to another room or if the ceiling is higher than average, the two-end fold-over is better.

For average ceiling height you may find a sturdy wooden box is handier than a stepladder for the paper application job. Just unfold the upper end (it peels open with no trouble) and stick it to the wall with half of the shift-and-match allowance at the top. Unless your house is a new one with room corners definitely vertical, you should have a pencil line on the wall to line up the first strip so you can be sure it's vertical. Some people hang a spoon on a string from a tack near the ceiling, and draw the line along the string—if the spoon ever stops swinging. It's a lot easier to draw the line with a carpenter's level. This is a handy tool to have, anyway, so there's no harm in buying it at a time when you can actually use it. Just be sure you get one with a plumb level in it. If you tell the hardware clerk what you want to do with it, he'll get you the right type. These levels have little glass tubes with liquid inside and a bubble that shows you when something is either perfectly horizontal or perfectly vertical. If you buy one let the clerk show you how it works. They're no trouble to use.

Once you stick the paper to the wall along the upper portion of the strip, it's easy to unfold the paste-to-paste lower section. The nice thing about the ready-made paste is its slipperiness. You can slide the paper enough to get it lined up with the vertical pencil line. But get the top portion lined up as well as possible right at the start so you don't have to do too much paper sliding. The risk in sliding the stuff around is in weakening the grip of the paste and in possibly pulling the paper so hard as to split it. An inch or two of sliding is usually simple enough.

SMOOTHING, TRIMMING, AND OTHER FINISHING TOUCHES

When the paper is on the wall, use the smoothing brush to work out any air bubble blisters by easing them toward the edge. Use the seam roller to get the edges down firm if they show any sign of rippling. The chances are you'll have very few problems in all of this. You'll be a little scared while you're putting up the first strip. But after you've put up about three strips, you're likely to decide you want to paper the whole house. If that's the way you feel, go ahead.

When the strip is all smoothed out, use a razor blade or a Stanley trimming knife to trim off the excess at top and bottom. (There are also sharp-edged wheel-like trimming tools for this.) Just work the paper into the corner between ceiling and wall and between wall and the top of the baseboard with your fingers. Then slide the trimming tool along the worked-in corner to trim it. Do the same around windows and doors. All along, work so you don't leave gaps that aren't covered by the new wallpaper.

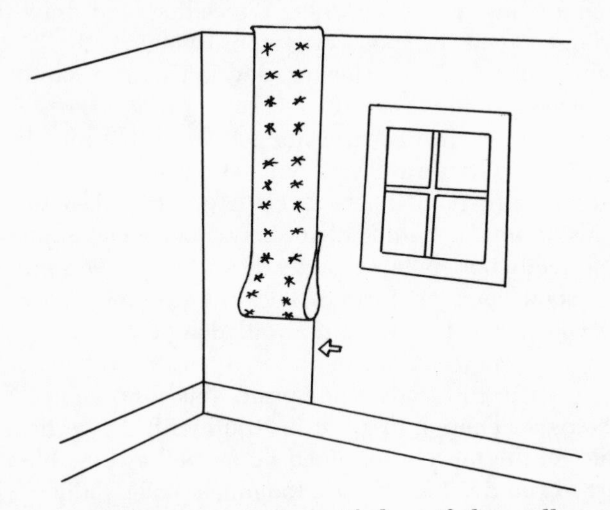

When you get to a room corner, it's best if the wallpaper strip goes around the corner a little way. If it happens to come exactly along the corner line, you can overlap the next strip slightly around the corner. Your eyes don't pick up the pattern carry-over so keenly at corners. The reason for avoiding seams at the corner line: when house foundations settle unevenly (as they often do), plaster or wallboard cracks are likely at corners. If the crack comes at a wallpaper seam, it's likely to make the seam open in flappy style. If the paper goes around the corner (even if it should split), it's not likely to be very obvious. If you have a new house this isn't likely to be worth worrying about. And if you have an old house that somebody has fixed up over the years, you can probably worry even less. Once a house has finished settling, it's likely to stay put.

Wipe off any squeezed-out wallpaper paste as you go along. A clean sponge with plain water does it. When the whole job is done, take a look around for any little seam ripples. If you've used the seam roller, you probably won't find any ripples. But

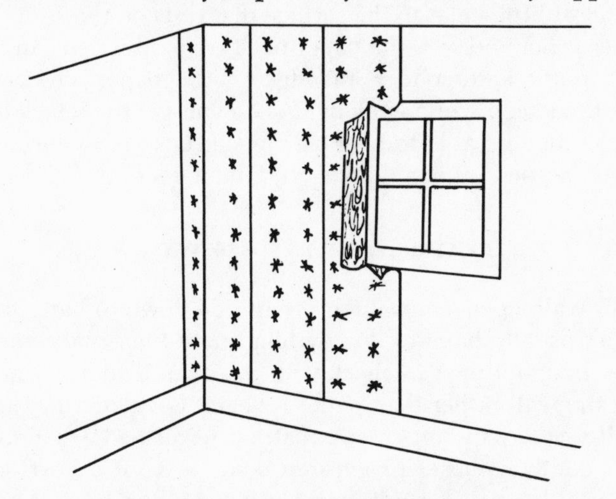

even if you do, they'll usually flatten down if you push a little paste under them with a dime-store artist's brush and follow up with the seam roller. If it should turn out that you have bungled in gruesome style and you have ripples and blisters that you can't flatten, there's still a way. You can razor-slit the ripple or blister along its peak and press the slit edges down so they overlap. The chances are nobody will ever notice it. But the best procedure is to work carefully in the first place.

WHEN TO REMOVE OLD WALLPAPER

Whether you plan to paint or paper a wall, if the wallpaper is loose in sizable areas, the chances are it's likely to loosen elsewhere. So you'll be better off removing it than try to make do.

The best bet for this job is a rented wallpaper removing tool. Most tool rental stores, like United Rent-Alls, have them. And, of course, you can get full instructions on the use of the thing where you rent it. Many rental stores offer bargain rates over week ends. But the rental fee is likely to be one of the lowest items on your list anyway. In general, these gadgets generate steam electrically or otherwise, and blow it (along with water vapor) against the paper. You just hold the flat side against the wall. The steam comes out of little holes in the surface that rests on the wall. Once the paper is hot and wet, the paper peels off easily. You can shove a broad putty knife under an edge of the paper to start the process, then keep working along. When you get the knack of the thing, you may be able to peel off big sheets of paper at a time. Whatever happens, if you do the job right, it goes fast.

TREATMENT OF EXPOSED WALL

If your wallpaper removal job brings you down to bare plaster, you won't usually have to do anything more than make sure it's smooth—though it pays to check with the paint dealer if you plan to paint the wall rather than paper it again. For papering, just go ahead. If you're papering a wall that has never had any finish on it, and it's either plaster or gypsum board, give it a coat of any water-mixed latex wall paint before you start the job. (Use a color close to the paper color.) This will make sure things stick. Otherwise your paste may be soaked up before it can do its job. One final tip: always ask questions that interest you—and ask them where you buy your materials.

9

RUGS, UPHOLSTERY, AND FLOOR COVERINGS

SOMETIMES, no matter how much they may have cost, it just isn't possible to protect your rugs and upholstery. You simply have the wrong kind of friends with the wrong kind of kids and the wrong kind of pets. Or maybe you were born sloppy.

Now and then you see the trouble coming, but it's too late to do anything about it. It could be in the form of a visit from Felicia Fogtop from down the street. She has her darling little boy Wellington with her and their pet poodle Pomade. Wellington is dragging an oversized toy truck behind him, holding a grimy oil can in his free hand, and chewing bubble gum.

Felicia tramps across your new oyster-white broadloom, plops onto the sofa, and yanks a bottle of Parisian Gory Red nail polish from her handbag. She'd rather do her nails in your place, she says, than in her own joint where everything is such a mess. Little Wellington grinds his dump truck across the rug, leaving a pair of parallel black tracks behind. You hear him grumbling about too much oil on the wheel bearings. And Felicia says her husband feels that a boy should learn about mechanical things like lubrication while he's young, but there's no need to waste money doing it. So Felicia's husband always fills the kid's oil can with old crankcase drainings.

You hear a whimper from Pomade, the poodle, just in time to see him leaving a corner of the room where a big wet area is spreading through the rug. That's when Felicia says she just remembered that she forgot to take Pomade for a walk before they drove down to see you. She's so upset she jumps up and tips over the coffee table and sends the bottle of Parisian Gory Red nail polish splattering on the carpet. This makes her cut loose with a banshee shriek that startles little Wellington so he coughs out his piece of bubble gum and steps on it. Frightened, he bumps his nose on the back of a chair, drops his oil can upside down, stumbles over the truck, and bleeds all the way to the front door. So Felicia gathers up the whole bunch and heads for home. And there you are. What do you do now?

Happily, the people who make rugs and carpets in various parts of the world have actually thought of situations something like this, and have worked out methods to help you set things right. To see how it all works, along with some additional helpful procedures, we might as well begin with the shambles created by Mrs. Fogtop and her little monsters.

SPILLS REQUIRE PROMPT TREATMENT

The first rule of carpet-and-rug rescue calls for quick action. Some calamities that might ruin a rug or carpet in five minutes may have almost no effect if remedial treatment begins within a minute. And this isn't as frantic as it sounds. You can travel to any part of the average house and back again within a minute.

NAIL POLISH REMOVAL

The Parisian Gory Red nail polish and young Wellington's bloody nose present the most urgent problem, as fleeting time tends to set them in the body of the carpet. (Wellington's blood, not his nose.) But the first aid in each case is easy, and the remedies are likely to be close at hand.

Pour cold water on the blood stains as quickly as possible, and start mopping them up with a clean absorbent rag or a sponge. Then pour on some more cold water so they won't dry. Pinch up as much of the spilled nail polish as possible with another rag, and don't spread the stuff with wipe-around motion. Just work the rag inward and upward, and have some nail polish remover handy. Use this to keep the remaining spilled polish from drying, and to make it easier to get up with the rags. (If you have the kind of carpet fiber that's dissolved by nail polish remover, you should know it—and send a replacement bill to Felicia.)

To remove the nail polish completely, you simply follow the same procedure on a bigger scale. To avoid sticking the carpet to the floor (if the stain is a large one), you'd better lift it at the stained area and shove some kind of box under it. If this calls for pulling some tacks, do it. You can finish the job with lacquer thinner, which costs less than polish remover. But turn out all pilot lights, don't smoke, and open the windows. The stuff you're working with on this job can burn like crazy, and under some conditions, explode.

When the stain seems to be gone, let the whole thing dry. Don't be surprised if the cleaned area looks a little different from the rest of the rug. A professional cleaning job may be necessary. But your quick action may have avoided utter ruin. Next time Felicia comes in with her nail polish throw her out before she uses it.

WHEN BLOOD STAINS SEEM STUBBORN

Water doesn't evaporate as fast as the acetone in lacquer thinner, so the water-doused bloody areas of your carpeting can wait a little longer for further attention. Just keep wetting the bloodstains and blotting them up with anything absorbent. Old terry-cloth towels are fine for this. And when you run out of towels you can use rags, and finally old newspapers. (Don't use new newspapers, especially early editions, as the printer's ink can smear off and add to your troubles.) You can help things along in the latter stages by adding just a little detergent—not enough to bubble up a batch of suds. And when the stain disappears, let the whole thing dry. Propping it up on a box, as for the nail polish job, speeds the drying. In case some trace of stain remains, a little liquid dry cleaner will usually eliminate it. All this fuss is based on a major blood-letting. For a cut-finger type blood spot, use the same procedure on a much smaller scale. The important points: start the cleanup before the stain dries, if possible. Use *only cold* water, and plenty of it. (Hot water sets blood stains.)

ANTIDOTE FOR PET DAMAGE

Treat pet-wet spots much the same as blood spots, dousing on cold water and blotting up. This thins out any tinge of color in the area, and by dilution, lessens the urine's alkalinity. After the initial clear-water dousing, water with a little detergent added helps the job along. To eliminate the chance of any aftereffects from the alkalinity, sponge the area with half a cup of white vinegar stirred thoroughly into a quart of warm (not hot) water. Let the solution soak in and work for a few minutes, then rinse with clear water, and blot up. If there's any visible urine stain, repeat the procedure until the stain vanishes. This diluted vinegar step is very important in cases where the pet-wet stain has dried before being discovered. Use *only* white vinegar, however, or you may make the stain worse.

The sad case of the sick dog

If a pet animal regurgitates food onto your rug, you are dealing with an acid, rather than an alkaline substance. So your treatment is different. Start by scraping up the solid material. A cardboard from a shirt returned from the laundry is a good tool for this. Tear the cardboard in half and use one half as a scoop, the other as a pusher. This is better than a tool like a trowel because you can throw the whole thing away. Once the solids are removed, follow up with the rinse and blot performance. If particles are embedded in the carpet pile, a scrubbing brush cleans them out, but scrub gently. When everything looks clean, neutralize the acid (from the animal's digestive juices) by sponging the area with an alkaline solution made by mixing a tablespoonful of baking soda or ammonia with a quart of water. If you use baking soda, make sure it is completely dissolved. Let it stand a few minutes to do its job, then blot it up. Finish with another clear-water rinse-and-blot performance.

Use the same neutralizing procedure for spilled fruit juice or other acids—like the fluid from Junior's auto battery, if he happens to lug it through the house for a basement checkup. But get to your neutralizing fast if a battery is the cause.

OILY SPOTS

Dirty oil stains like Wellington's truck tracks, are sometimes easier to handle than clean oil dribbles. You can see the dirty ones, so you can work on them. The clean oil drip may be hard to find—but it will start collecting dust and dirt just the same. The first step depends on the substance. If it's something gloppy like thick salad dressing or soft butter, scrape up as much as possible to get things started. Then use a good dry cleaning fluid (some are made especially for rugs) to complete the job. You can eliminate the old-time fire hazard by using a nonflammable cleaning fluid, and you can avoid most of the vapor-inhalation risk by *not* using a carbon tetrachloride (often called carbon tet) type of cleaner. Although carbon tet doesn't burn and does a fine cleaning job, its vapor, when inhaled for a while, can cause serious injury to various organs, including the liver. So today's cleaning fluids are formulated with other solvents to a large extent, such as the trichloroethane in Carbona. These solvents are often rated as much as twenty times safer than the old carbon tet. (The carbon tet, however, is still used in many professional operations where proper safety precautions are followed to the letter.) Whatever cleaning fluid you use, be sure to provide adequate ventilation. For big jobs, open several windows, and if there's no breeze, let a small fan blow the vapor away.

If it's possible to flex the rug so you can slide a cleaner-moistened cloth against the strands of carpet pile at the rim of the stain, pushing inward toward the stain's center, you can avoid much of the ring problem. The ring results from dissolved stain or spot material soaking outward from the original stain. If you do end up with a ring, dampen it with the cleaner and blend it out in both directions to remove as much soil as possible and reduce the contrast between the ring and the rest of the carpet.

Two important precautions in dry cleaning carpet: don't use

the cleaning fluid so generously it will soak through to the rubber backing of the rug—if the rug has such a backing. This may damage the backing. And because of the wide differences in modern synthetic fibers, try the cleaning fluid on a sample piece of the carpet (if you happen to have a sample) before you use it on the carpet itself. Otherwise try it on a dime-sized area that's hidden under a piece of furniture. If the carpet color comes off on the cleaning cloth, or if you notice any other unwanted effect, don't tackle the big job with the cleaner. If you're in doubt, check with the manufacturer of the carpet. In general, however, established brands of dry cleaning fluid are likely to be safe.

If you can't eliminate a ring after dry-cleaning a grease spot, your best bet is a complete rug shampoo. You can do this yourself with one of the preparations made for the purpose. You don't have to take the rug up from the floor. You can do it the hard way by crawling all over the rug, sponge in hand, pot of shampoo beside you. Or you can speed the job and spare your knees and back with a long-handled rug shampoo applicator. You can buy one of these things for the price of a good roast. And many of them can be used on furniture upholstery, too.

BUBBLE GUM WILL COME OFF

The same cleaning fluid that removes the grease or oil stains will remove chewing gum (bubble gum or otherwise) from your rugs—and from your upholstery. Scrape or pull out as much as you can, first, but don't work so hard that you pull the pile out of the rug with it. Soften the gum that remains on the strands of pile by holding a cleaner-moistened cloth between thumb and forefinger, and pinching the cloth so as to grip the gummy strands between the folds. Hold the cloth there for a moment, then slide it gently upward to slide off the gum. You may have to repeat this process a number of times to clear the whole mess.

DON'T CRY OVER SPILLED MILK

The younger your offspring the better the chance that your rug will get an occasional slosh of milk. Don't use soap to clean it up.

A little detergent in water does the job better. Give it a sponge rinse with clear water afterward, and mop up, to get rid of any sediment that might turn rancid.

RUST

Rust isn't a common enemy of carpeting, but when it does leave its ruddy mark, about all you can do safely is tackle it with a sponge and water and a little detergent. Although chemical rust removers are available, some types may also remove the color from the pile, or even remove the pile. So if it won't sponge off, call a rug cleaner and let him worry about it.

HOW TO TACKLE CIGARETTE BURNS

You can avoid this type of damage by keeping an eye on your ash trays. But sometime one of those teetering incendiaries may tumble onto the rug when you're not looking. If it burns itself out while resting on the tips of the carpet pile, the remedy may be surprisingly easy. Just clip off the charred ends of the pile or tufts, removing as little as possible. Then sponge the area with water and a little detergent, and finish with a clear-water rinse. Never let the person who caused the trouble know it was that easy to fix.

If the cigarette burns all the way down to the backing, you can have the rug repaired professionally if your carpet dealer can match the fiber. Or, if you have rug-making talent, you may be able to do the repair job yourself—if you can get the fiber in the right color. Send the bill to the person who caused the damage. At least, that'll keep him from coming back.

How to ruin a carpet completely

One of the easiest ways to make a total wreck of a beautiful rug or carpet is by dumping India ink or other indelible ink on it. Ordinary writing ink won't do. You can usually wash that out of the rug simply by repeated cold-water sloshing and blotting. Certain red wines are also excellent rug wreckers, especially if the rug is of a light color. The safest rule: don't tote indelible ink around carpeted rooms. And if you like red wine, use red rugs to match. Or switch to gin.

RENEWING COLORS IN ORIENTAL RUGS

It takes a long time to wear a real Oriental rug down to the backing, but it can happen. Except in extreme cases, however, some of the pile is still there. But the backing shows through and you have a very obvious worn spot. If you're a wealthy world traveler, you can have the rug sent back to the land where it was made, and restored by the artisans who produced it. More than one millionaire has done it. If you're not quite so well-heeled, however, you can do a surprisingly good job of faking the restoration yourself. This calls for touching up the backing (where it shows through) with aniline dyes that match the color of the pile. You can do it with dime-store artists' brushes and it's not nearly as tricky as it sounds. A quick-penetrating dye like North American Dye Company's Colorama (which contains a detergent to aid penetration) is a good choice for the work. This type is available in more than one hundred colors that can be intermixed to create an almost limitless color range. To prepare for the job, you can get a color chart from the company for about a dollar. (If your dye order is above a certain amount, the dollar is refunded.)

You can play safe by making the hot-water dye mix a little lighter than the color to be matched—for the first try. Then add a little more dye powder to bring the colors closer. In case you go overboard, the same company makes a color remover that takes out the dye and lets you start over again. So you can't miss. The best method: do the touch-up in a good light. Then stand a few feet away to see how it looks. The colors change slightly as the rug backing dries. If this calls for a little more touch-up, just apply more dye to the areas that need it. Jigger glasses make good containers for the small amounts of different colors you'll be using. But keep them on a tray with a high rim around it in case you spill some. (You can't take spilled dye out of a rug without risk of taking out the old dye, too.) When your touch-up job is done, of course, you'll still have most of the dye left, as touch-up requires very little. You can use it on anything from blankets to overcoats, and also on wood.

REMOVING STAINS FROM UPHOLSTERY

You use the same general methods and materials in cleaning upholstery as in cleaning rugs and carpets. And you take the same precautions. If, for example, a smeared-up sofa has foam rubber cushioning, avoid using dry cleaning fluids so liberally as to soak through into the rubber, as it can damage it just as it can damage rubber rug backing. This is no reflection on the cleaning fluid.

REPAIRING A BURN

Cigarette burns in upholstery present a different problem from the same damage on rugs, as they're likely to burn all the way through the fabric. The result may be a long-smoldering conflagration inside the stuffing. You often read about this kind of thing in the headlines after a house burns down. The danger lies in the fact that the slow combustion may linger for hours before it breaks into open flame. So, if you find a cigarette burn through upholstery on a piece of furniture, you'll do well to shoot some water through the hole and place the piece outside until you can be sure it's not a time bomb.

It's not always possible to repair a cigarette burn in upholstery without redoing the entire piece. But if you can reach the inside of the hole, and if you can snip a large enough piece from a tacked-under area to make a patch, you may be able to save the day. (You sometimes find a little spare fabric under chairs and sofas where the upholstery is tacked to the wood frame.) While sewing a patch in place would call for a surgeon's touch to avoid puckers and wrinkles, you may be able to do it with Pliobond adhesive (See p. 162 "Buna-N Adhesive"). To apply it properly, coat a margin around the inside of the hole with the adhesive, and coat a matching margin around the rim of the patch. Then push the patch in place, and smooth it out. The patch should be on the inside of the upholstery. If you get it out of line, you can soften the adhesive by passing an electric iron over the patched area (on the outside) so you can pull the patch free and try again. The job is easy on a slip cover, and easiest of all when the patched area is dark-colored. The dark color makes even a sloppy job less apparent.

An important point to remember

Whatever you're cleaning or repairing, keep in mind that the completed job is much more noticeable to you than to anybody else. You know just where it is, so you can spot it at a glance. You can see the ring from the cleaning fluid, the slightly different tone. You know some particular area of your rug or your sofa is just a little lighter because it had a good dry cleaning after you scooped up a couple of smoked oysters and an anchovy. But nobody else knows where to look, so they're not at all likely to notice it unless you're clunk-headed enough to tell them about it. So once you've fixed the thing up, keep your mouth shut about it.

THE NEW SLICK FLOOR COVERINGS

Linoleum, vinyl, rubber, asphalt tile, and the rest of the modern assortment, are a little less nerve-wracking when something terrible happens. If you spill something alarming like concentrated bleach or paint remover on them, the most important point is to mop it up as quickly as possible. Don't leave it there while you listen to a long-winded phone call. Just tell Arabella you'll call her back. This is especially important when something oily or some petroleum solvent spills on asphalt tile. If something sticky (especially if it's hot) lands on this kind of floor covering, scrape it off immediately with a putty knife or the nearest thing to it. Then use the type of cleaner that matches the floor covering. These cleaners are not interchangeable from one type of covering to another—so keep the right kind on hand. If the spillage has left a film the putty knife can't remove, follow up with number 0 steel wool, rubbing the area smooth. Dip the steel wool in the cleaner recommended for the floor covering. Then rinse the whole business—but only with water or a rinse specified by the floor covering manufacturer. Because of the wide variation in the chemical make-up of today's floor coverings, your best bet is to get complete maintenance instructions where you buy the material—and use the floor-care product the manufacturer specifies. A polish that can make one type of floor beautiful may ruin another.

GENERAL TIPS

A final, general tip on all types of floor covering, including rugs and carpets, might well be along the same line. Get detailed instructions on the care of any and all floor coverings when and where you buy them. And keep the instruction pamphlets where you can find them. Some modern rugs, for example, are made of fibers that are damaged or discolored by alkaline liquids, yet their backing may be of another fiber that can be damaged by acid. Then somebody spills a strong acid on the rug. The label on the container tells you to neutralize it with something alkaline. But the rug pamphlet tells you not to use any such thing on it. So what do you do? Rug manufacturers and professional rug cleaners wish there were a simple, pat answer. The best solution, of course, is to avoid slopping awful things on your floor coverings. But if it happens, you'll have to use your own judgment. Complete flooding with plain water dilutes most of the acid and alkaline things likely to spill on your rugs. And a gentle neutralizing of one with the other can usually be managed. If you want to be sure of the effect of the cures you may someday have to use, try them in advance on scraps of the same floor covering.

10

HOW TO HANG THINGS ON WALLS

ALMOST every time you hang up something or fasten something to something else, there's some kind of load to be carried—and there's a right way of doing the job. When you hang a picture, for example, you can drive a little nail into the plaster to hold the picture if it doesn't weigh much. But you'll be better off using a picture hook because it's much less likely to pull out of the wall. And if you want to hang a heavy mirror, you not only need the right kind of hanger, but you'll have to find a stud (wooden post inside the wall) to drive the hanger into, so it won't pull out of the plaster.

HANGING A PICTURE

This job starts with the problem of how to get it where you want it.

If there's nothing on the back of the picture frame to fasten a piece of string or wire on for the job, buy some very small screw eyes from a large hardware store. (You won't usually find these at the dime store.) You can put one of these into each side of the picture frame at the back, not more than a third of the way down from the top of the frame. (If they're farther down, the frame will tip outward too much at the top.) Measure the distance on each side so the screw eyes are the same distance from the top. Then fasten a piece of strong string or thin wire from one screw eye across to the other with enough slack in it so you can push the middle of the string about half the distance to the top before it pulls taut. With the string or wire taut, snag the picture hook under the center of it just the way it will be with the picture on the wall. Then measure up from the bottom of the frame to the picture hook's nail or pin—taking your measurement close against the picture hook. All you have to do now is get somebody to hold the picture against the wall where you think you want it.

When you hang a picture simply fasten the wire to screw eyes in the upper third of the frame and stretch wire or cord to the picture hook. Measure from pin of picture hook to bottom of picture frame. Then use that distance to space the picture hook above the bottom-of-frame pencil mark when you get ready to mount the picture hook.

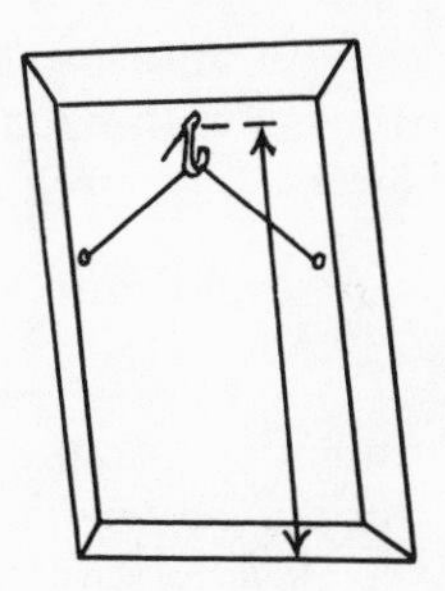

Stand away from it and see how it looks. If it's right, make a light pencil mark under the center of the bottom of the frame, and lay the picture and frame aside. Measure up from the pencil mark the same distance you measured earlier from the frame bottom to the picture hook pin with the wire pulled taut. This gives you the exact spot to drive your picture hook. When you hang your picture, it will be where you want it. Not higher, not lower. If you do manage to goof, you can still raise or lower the picture by shortening the wire or lengthening it.

HANGING HEAVY OBJECTS

The procedure for hanging a heavy picture or mirror is just the same, but you have to find a stud inside the wall first. The easiest way to find the stud nearest the location you want is by tapping the wall lightly with a small hammer or the handle of a screwdriver while holding the screwdriver by the blade. When you tap between studs, you hear a hollow sound. When you are over the stud, the sound is distinctly solid. To confirm the location of the stud, you can drive a small finishing nail through the wall into the stud. If the nail slips in freely after penetrating about half an inch, you've missed the stud. Pull the nail out and insert a bent piece of thin wire. By tipping the wire around you can locate the stud to one side of it or the other. Then drive the nail again, and it should hit the stud. Actually, in most cases you'll hit the stud with the first shot, as the sound-tapping is pretty accurate. There are, as you may have seen in ads and hardware stores, a variety of stud locators. Certain kinds of walls, however, can sometimes foil these gadgets. So if you're not likely to do a lot of stud locating, you might as well do it by tapping.

MOUNTING DRAPERY HARDWARE

Fortunately, drapery hardware is designed to be mounted directly on the wooden trim around the windows, so you don't have to do any stud hunting. Even if you want your drapes to ride on long traverse rods that extend well beyond the sides of the window trim, you can buy hardware that supports it all from the trim. The Kirsch Company, of Sturgis, Michigan, is one manufacturer of this type of drapery hardware. As the wooden window trim is nailed to the 2 x 4 studding and other wall framing, you don't have to worry about heavyweight drapes pulling the hardware loose.

11

DOORS, WINDOWS, LOCKS, AND CATCHES

THE THINGS that are supposed to open and close around your house, with or without keys, don't always do what they're supposed to. Sliding doors skitter off the track. Some doors stick and won't open. Others rattle and bang. And sometimes knobs come off in your hand or keys won't work—always when you're in a hurry. Or the window is jammed shut just when you want to roar and yell at that big goon of a hound dog that's digging up your tulip bulbs. Fortunately you can usually fix whatever it is that needs fixing, even under nightmarish circumstances.

WHEN A KNOB COMES OFF

The doorknob that comes off in your hand isn't too nerve-wracking unless you're outside in the pouring rain trying to get in to answer the ringing phone. You try to put the knob back on the little square shaft, but the little square shaft just slips farther and farther into the door, and the knob won't go on it. The key works, but you can't open the door without the knob. You have no tools. Where do you go from here?

You may have the tools in your pocket. If you have a thin dime, a nail file, or a pocketknife, or all three, you have a good chance of opening the door in a matter of a quarter of a minute or so. Use the nail file or the thin dime to loosen the screw in the hub of the knob. (You can do it with a knife blade, but it's not as easy.) Then pull the square shaft out as far as it will come. Push the butt end of the nail file or the blade of the knife firmly against the shaft right up against the door, so it won't slip in again, and put the knob back on the shaft. Once the hub screw is loosened, some

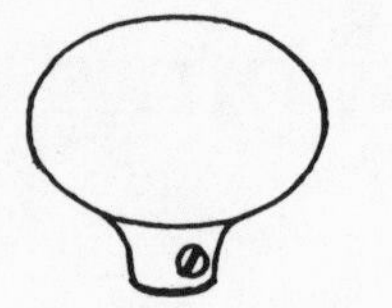

The important screw in a doorknob is located in the hub, as shown.

knobs simply slide on to the shaft; others must be turned in a clockwise direction to screw them on like a nut on a bolt. As soon as the knob is on the shaft, tighten the screw, turn the knob, open the door, and get in there and answer the phone.

STICKING DOORS ARE EASY TO FIX

The door that won't open, or almost won't open, usually gives you a hint as to how to open it. When you turn the knob and yank, where does the door stick? If it springs out at the top corner on the knob side, but sticks at the bottom, try heaving up on the knob as hard as you can while pulling on it. This often works so well you'll be caught off balance as the thing opens. If it's stuck at the top, just bear down on the knob. It doesn't matter too much whether the actual sticking is along the *bottom edge* or *top edge* or along the vertical edge at the top or bottom. Just push up or down on the knob, as described, and you'll usually get the door open. (Fortunately there's enough play in most hinges and their fastenings to allow a little movement.)

Once the door is open (if it's your own), take a look at the edges to see where it was sticking. Fairly obvious rub marks usually tell you at a glance—unless they're on the top or bottom edge. If they're on the vertical edge, you can usually shave off enough wood from the sticking portion with a block plane (see Chapter 2), without taking the door off the hinges. (Purists scream at this, even when it's a cinch.) If you have to take the door off, you'll be surprised to find it's really not much of a job, but a helper comes in handy to lend a hand in lifting the door free.

WHEN THE HINGE IS AT FAULT

Most door hinges have removable pins (the vertical shafts) that can be taken out by tapping them up from the bottom with a hammer, then lifting them out from the top. If they're caked with paint, you know they're stuck only along half their length because one half of the hinge moves when you open the door. So relax. Usually you can tap them all the way up from the bottom anyway, using a nail set (Chapter 2) to reach up inside for the latter part of the job. In extreme cases you can oil them with nail polish remover to soften the seeped-in paint. If they're rusted, use the same substance (Liquid Wrench) that mechanics use on rusted nuts and bolts. You can buy this at hardware stores. In most cases, however, you won't have to face such headaches.

In the rare case of a door whose hinges do not have removable pins, take the screws out of the sides of the hinges that attach to the door jamb, not the ones that attach to the door. This usually makes it a little easier when you put the door back in again. Whether you're removing hinge pins or screws, start with the bottom hinge and finish with the top. This way the weight of the door presses inward and holds together the loosened hinges. If you do it the other way, the door may tip outward and bend the lower hinges out of shape, making the job a lot harder.

Once the door is freed, set it down on its hinged edge with something under it to keep it from scratching the floor. Look for the rub marks that call for planing. If you have to plane over a corner of the door, *always* plane *inward* over the corner onto the edge. If you do it the other way, the plane blade will tend to split slivers of wood outward from the corner on most doors. The reason: the way most door parts are joined at corners, the grain of the cross members at top and bottom is at right angles to the grain of the vertical edge. If this isn't clear, forget it. But always plane inward over the corners anyway. If the hinges were stuck by paint or rust, clean them up. Then it's easier to try the door after you've shaved off a little at the rub points. Just hook up the top and bottom hinges for the test fittings. If the door still sticks after a trial, shave off a little more and try it again. When it fits, quit shaving, and hook up all the hinges for keeps. It's a good idea to paint the shaved areas to minimize moisture absorption by the wood in humid weather. But don't glop on so much paint you get everything stuck again.

Once in a while door-sticking is entirely the fault of the hinges. When it is, however, you can tell by the large amount of play when you heave up or press down on the knob. (You feel it most on the heave-up.) The trouble is caused more often by loose screws through the hinges into the wood than by poor hinges. You can usually see which screws are loose. If they become snug and tight when you turn them in with a screwdriver, that's all it takes to get things working right. If they just keep turning but never get tight, a simple trick fixes them. But don't take them all out at once. Remove one screw at a time and replace it before removing the next one. With the screw removed, coat a wooden toothpick with household cement (like Duco cement in tubes), push it all the way into the hole, and break it off flush with the hinge surface. Then turn the screw back into the hole. The toothpick usually makes it fit tightly enough to draw in snug and tight. If it still slips, add an extra toothpick. Once the screw is seated and tight, don't force it any farther or you may break it loose again.

DOORS THAT WON'T CATCH OR LOCK

When a door won't catch, take a look at the stop strip around the door jamb. This is the little wooden strip the door bumps against when it closes. If the door and the strip swell a little from excessive humidity, or if a stray tack or a wad of Junior's chewing gum happens to be wedged against the edge of the strip, there's trouble. The bevel-ended latch bolt that sticks out of the door latch can't get in quite far enough to pop into the little square hole in the shiny brass strike plate on the door jamb. So the door doesn't catch. A warped door that hits at a corner before it closes completely can cause the same trouble.

If the trouble is as simple as a stray tack or gum wad, just remove the obstruction and all's well. If it's the result of swelling or warping, it's not too practical to attack the cause directly. (It's not easy to unswell or unwarp a door.) And removing and relocating the stop strip is a lot of fuss. It's much easier to remove the strike plate and file the hole in it a little bigger so the latch bolt can pop into it even when everything's swollen. You need file only the side of the hole *away* from the stop strip. In a sense, you are moving the hole outward so the door doesn't have to close quite so far in order for the latch bolt to pop in. The reason for filing the hole rather than moving the whole strike plate: you couldn't move the strike plate far enough to permit new holes for its screws. If you moved it that far, you'd be moving it too far.

A flat mill bastard file about 4 inches long is usually right for the job. (A longer file would be too wide for the hole.) You needn't blush when you ask the hardware clerk for the file. A flat mill bastard is a flat file with single-cut teeth across it. These are just fine, sharp, parallel grooves, like corduroy. (If they criss-crossed another bunch of grooves they'd be called second-cut.) The single-cut mill file teeth are handy for odd job filing because they leave a smooth surface. The word bastard, as far as files are concerned, simply indicates a tooth coarseness around the medium range.

To do the filing job right, you should grip the strike plate in some sort of vise, so this is a good time to buy one. You can get small ones that clamp on a table or shelf. Before you start the filing job, look carefully at the rub marks on the strike plate where the latch bolt has moved across it. If it looks as though the bolt is above or below the hole it's supposed to pop into, you may have to file the top or bottom edge of the hole in addition to the edge away from the stop strip. Sometimes you can confirm this too high or too low business by heaving up on the knob as you shut the door, or by pressing down on it. If the door latch catches properly when you heave up on the knob as you close it, you know you should file away a little of the lower edge of the hole in the strike plate. If it catches when you bear down on the knob, you should take a little off the upper edge of the hole. Doors get this way for various reasons. A little sag in the door itself, sloppiness in the hinges, even uneven settling of the house, can sometimes shift things enough to cause trouble.

When a door won't lock, it may have the same kind of ailment as one that doesn't catch. Open the door and turn the key in the lock. If the dead latch bolt moves in and out when you turn the key, there's nothing wrong with the lock itself. But if the key won't turn all the way when the door is closed you know the lock bolt is hitting an edge of the hole in the strike plate instead of sliding into the hole the way it's supposed to. So give it the same general filing treatment as described previously. You can tell which edge of the hole is being hit by painting the end of the bolt, then closing the door and turning the key so the bolt hits the strike plate. You'll see a little fresh paint where the bolt hits.

WHEN DOORS RATTLE AND ARE DRAFTY

Doors that rattle on windy days tell you several things. For one, your house has some sizable air leaks. And for another, your rattling doors don't fit too well. One of the best ways to stop windy-day door rattle is by weather stripping. If the rattling door is inside the house, between rooms, you can use a strip of weather stripping across the top only, fastened to the wooden stop strip. One of the handiest kinds of do-it-yourself weather stripping consists of a thin wood strip with a felt or foam plastic edge on it. You fasten it to the door jamb's stop strip so that the felt or soft plastic presses lightly against the door when it's closed. Sometimes you get an envelope of little skinny nails with the weather stripping for the fastening job. Otherwise you can buy them at the same hardware store. Be sure they're long enough to go through the wooden part of the weather stripping and at least an equal distance (preferably a little more) into the wooden stop strip. There are two common types of little skinny nails. The ones with flat heads are called wire nails, and the ones with almost invisible knoblike heads are called brads, and are easier to conceal. You can use either kind for weather stripping. You'll probably want them in about ¾-inch or 1-inch length.

Doors that are drafty also need weather stripping, but they need it all the way around. Use the same weather stripping but run it up the stop strips on both sides of the door as well as across the top. There's a different, wider type, made especially to use across the bottom of the door. Ask for this where you buy the other kind. The complete job does more for you than you may realize. If you add up the area of a ⅛-inch crack around a door, you'll be surprised to find that it equals a hole big enough to shove your fist through. Add up similar cracks around all the outside doors and windows in your house and you actually have an area as big as a fair-sized window—open all the time. So when you seal all these cracks, you really close a window you never knew was open. And the saving in heating fuel may easily pay for the weather stripping in the first month or so. Many new homes are already weather stripped when you move in. Others are not. And some are weather stripped so badly you think you're living in a cave anyway. The real test: if you feel drafts around windows and doors you need weather stripping. Sometimes it's so bad your curtains wiggle on windy days. The same general type of weather stripping you use on doors does the job on windows, too. But tell the hardware clerk what you want the stripping for. Some types are made in window-size packages that minimize waste. (You cut the stuff to length with a pocketknife or wood saw.) There are also flexible strippings that are especially handy for rounded or odd-shaped windows and doors. And they can be used on standard ones, too.

SLIDING DOORS THAT JUMP THE TRACK

Most sliding doors ride on little wheels at the top only, and are kept in place at the bottom usually by three little floor guides—one at the center of a two-door unit, and one at each side. There are also a few continuous track types.

The usual cause of track-jumping (at the top) is some obstruction on the floor. A box or a jumble of shoes, for example, can not only stop the bottom of the door in mid-travel, but pitch it sideways, too. If the door is traveling forward to close, this tends to lift the rear track wheel at the top and push it crosswise off the track at the same time. If the rig is a lightweight economy model, the track may flex enough to let the wheel slip completely out of the groove, and you're all jammed up. What many people do next to get the thing back on the track sometimes wrecks it completely. They call for the biggest ape in the house, and with much heaving and grunting, force everything back in place. The result often is bent track, loosened wheels, and a general mess. If you want to do it right, take the screws out of the floor guides so you can tilt the door and put the wheel back on the track without forcing anything. (That's the way the door was mounted in the first place.) Then let the door dangle back to vertical position, slip the floor guides back where they were, and put the screws back in their original holes. Then arrange the junk on the floor of the closet so it won't knock the door off the track.

If your sliding doors sail off the track without anything knocking them off, they simply weren't installed right—and it happens often in this day of ever-increasing intelligence. In fact, one prospective home buyer was knocked flat on the floor when a bevy of high-styled fruitwood doors disengaged themselves from a spacious closet and landed on top of her. If this happens to you, take a look at the manufacturer's name on the wheel hangers or track, send for an assembly instruction sheet, and put the whole business together right. If you can't get the specific instructions, you can undoubtedly do the job by following some simple principles that apply to sliding doors in general.

First, the track at the top and the guides at the bottom should be mounted so the clearance at the bottom is just enough for free, easy sliding movement of the doors. You don't want so much clearance that the doors can tip noticeably. If they can, a sudden blocking impact at the bottom has a much better chance of lifting a wheel all the way out of the track. The best way to size up the original installation job: stand inside the closet with a good light and watch the whole thing operate. See if you can work it off the track without forcing it even slightly. In many types you'll find an adjustment on the wheel hangers to raise or lower the door slightly. Although this is intended for use in getting the door edges vertical, it can often be used to stop track-jumping, too. If the whole works is cheap and flimsy, however, with springy track and wobbly wheels, your best bet is to replace it.

WEATHER STRIPPING FOR DIFFERENT TYPES OF WINDOWS

You can't expect even the world's finest windows to stop every breath of air. You may not know it, but a considerable amount of outside air manages to get through even the walls of a house, and heating engineers have to include it in their calculations. In short, you don't live in a submarine. If your windows let in enough air to make a noticeable draft, however, it's time to do something about it. As the condition is more common in very old houses than in new ones, the means of curing it have been around for a long time. And the job is uncomplicated. Just tell your hardware store or lumberyard about your troubles, and you'll be shown an assortment of weather stripping that can do the job. Most of them can be fastened in place with brads in a few minutes. The important point to keep in mind is that of providing reasonable, but not excessive, pressure between the stripping and the window. Set your weather strip to bear gently against the window—especially if sliding motion is involved, as in the case of double-hung (slide up and down) windows. And don't install weather stripping on windows that have just been painted and still show any signs of tackiness. If a tacky surface remains in unmoved contact with some types of weather stripping, it may rip off a layer of the stuff when it's moved to open or close it. Read the instructions on the weather stripping package before you buy it so you'll be sure it can do the job you want. If you have doubts, or if the instructions are very brief, try squashing the weather stripping against something if it's to be used in a compression situation, as on casement windows—where the window squeezes the stripping as it closes. If there's a sliding motion, as in double-hung types, try sliding the stripping along a surface comparable to the one on the window. If all goes well, buy it. That's the best you can do, anyway, and the chances are you bought your house and your car with less advance checking. Most weather stripping can be painted to match the windows or doors, but avoid slopping paint on the plastic foam or sponge portions if there are any. The same applies to felt.

REPLACING BROKEN WINDOW GLASS

If you have a broken window on the first floor, you should be able to fix it without much trouble. If it's on the second floor, just be sure you don't break your neck doing the job. It's not really worth the risk, and, unless you're accustomed to working on ladders, call a pro. And make sure he has insurance of the proper type, or that your insurance covers him in case he falls on his head. (This insurance is something many homeowners never think about. But it pays to check with your agent before you hire anybody to do potentially risky work. You might possibly lose your shirt in a lawsuit.)

USING POINTS AND PUTTY THE PROFESSIONAL WAY

If the putty that holds the cracked or broken window pane into the wooden frame is hard and cracking, it's no trouble to pry out with a slim screwdriver, or better, with a chisel—if you happen to have one. Either way, it clicks out easily. If the putty is still soft, you'll probably find a beer opener the handiest tool for removing it. As you remove putty from the window frame, you'll uncover little metal triangles here and there. These are called points, and are driven into the wood frame close to the glass to help hold it in place. Save them. You can use them when you put the new pane in. But it's a good idea, too, to buy a little box of these things for use in replacing future broken windows.

Once the putty and the points are removed, put on some kind of tough gloves like work gloves, and take the glass out of the window frame. Usually this is a quick procedure. If you have any trouble, however, just let yourself go and whack it out with a hammer. But protect yourself (especially your face) from flying pieces.

If the window is a standard size, you can simply buy a new pane to fit. If it's a little off-size you can buy it anyway, but you may have to wait about two minutes while the hardware clerk or lumberyard clerk cuts it to the size you need. Either way, it's not likely to cost enough to shock you. If you have to take the broken pane out on a Sunday in an area where you can't buy a replacement until Monday, cut one of those laundered-shirt cardboards to fit in the meantime. A little cellulose tape, tacks, brads, or almost anything will hold it in place. When you get the glass, simply pull out the cardboard, put the glass in its place, and tap those metal triangular points in place to hold it. You can get a little bent-metal tool that lets you tap them in with a hammer. If this thing doesn't come with the box of points you buy, ask about it. For the average-sized pane you need only a couple of points to a side. For big panes, space the points at about the same gaps. Slide the hammer along the glass to tap the little tool that drives the points.

Once the pane is in place with the points holding it, you're ready for the putty—or one of the glazing compounds. They're all designed to stick to wood and glass more than they stick to the putty knife. Buy them at hardware stores or lumberyards. Generally, buy only enough for the job at hand, as you may find the stuff too hard to use after you save it for a few months. If you have leftover putty or glazing compound, you may be able to use it up constructively on other readily accessible windows where sections of putty have fallen out. This may save you the price of a hamburger and make you feel thrifty. And it's likely to cut your heating bills by eliminating air leaks you wouldn't bother about if you weren't trying to use up the glazing compound.

How to putty a window

Now that we've taken care of the leftovers, let's look into the matter of puttying up the new window pane. Professionals use a technique that requires experience. If you watch them work, you'll see them sweep the putty on like butter. But they know how to fix up the putty or whatever they're using so it has just the right consistency. (You can't butter bread with ice-cold, hard butter.)

Your best bet is to use your putty or glazing compound while it's fresh and easy to use. Look at the other panes of the window, and aim to get it on so it looks the same. Scrap it off the putty knife onto the frame around the glass. Then smooth it by sliding the slanted tip of the putty knife along it. If it pulls out anywhere, push it in again with the putty knife or your fingers. If it won't stick to the wood, it's probably because the wood has no paint on it, and it soaks up the solvent in the glazing compound. So if the wood looks bare when you whack the old broken glass out, give it a coat of primer and leave it overnight while the cardboard takes the place of the original glass.

All in all, the object of the putty job is to hold the window pane in place and to seal the seam around it. Keep that in mind and make the job as neat as you can. The chances are you can do a very good job. Millions of people have. As a final tip, in case you have to handle a fairly large piece of glass, dull the edges of the glass before you start working with it. Just fold a medium-grit piece of aluminum oxide abrasive paper (from the hardware store) over the edge of the glass and slide it back and forth a few times. This takes off the sharp edges if you do it right. Then use the same abrasive paper to take the keen point off the corners of the glass. From there on you can handle the glass without bloody consequences. But check the edges. After you know how to do this, it makes many glass jobs safer.

You should finish off your puttying job by painting the putty, preferably a few days later. If you slop paint on the glass, don't worry about it. You'll usually make more of a mess trying to wipe it off. And if you try to paint an entire window made of small panes without getting any on the glass, you'll have a long, tricky job. So just let it get on the glass where it can't be avoided, let it dry thoroughly, and scrape it off with one of those little gadgets that paint stores sell for the purpose. These are among the cheapest tools you'll ever buy, and they're good. The actual scraping is done by a standard razor blade that's held in the little tool by a clamping screw. When it gets dull, you simply replace the blade with a new one.

12

OUTSIDE THE HOUSE

NOBODY has to tell you about exterior paints, grass seed, or weed killers. It's all in the ads, the hardware stores, and just about everywhere else. But how do you get hold of a pile of mud or rocks, and how do you get rid of a big splashy puddle that forms on your lawn every time it rains? You don't see ads for mud, rocks, or puddle eliminators.

FILL FOR EVERY PURPOSE

How to buy mud. Contractors don't use the word mud. When a power shovel fills a truck with earth, they call it fill if it's ordinary clay, rocks, and sand. If it's from a gravel bank, they call it bank-run gravel, but it still looks more like mud. If it's the kind of rich earth that things grow in, they call it topsoil. Which one you buy depends on the job you want it to do. If you have a big, ugly hollow somewhere on your lawn, you can fill it with the cheapest kind of fill you can get. This is the kind that contractors are sometimes overloaded with after they've scooped out the basements for a shopping center.

To locate the man with the lowest price, look in your telephone book's yellow pages under "contractors, excavating," and call more than one, but not those far away. The farther the truck has to bring the material, the more it costs.

WHAT KIND OF FILL TO BUY

If you want to lengthen your driveway or add a parking area next to it, bank-run gravel is the material you want for the base. The sand, rocks, and claylike material in this make it pack down hard and firm. You don't need a steam roller. Just let it sit there for a month or so, or, better, drive your car back and forth over it to pack it. All this, if you're going to cover it with the fine-crushed stone some folks call driveway gravel. (Usually it's technically termed ½-inch crushed stone.) If you're planning a blacktop finish on a large area, it's possible to apply it yourself and pound it down. But you'll be wiser to let a pro do the whole job for you from base to surface. If you attempt it by hand, you're likely to get fed up before you finish the job. And you can't do it as well as a pro who has power equipment anyway.

Where tree roots are exposed (because soil has washed away), and where things just don't grow in spite of all your efforts, you probably need topsoil. The less rocks and foreign matter in this, the better. But the usual way of finding it is either by calling contracting firms or scanning classified for-sale ads in your local paper (if you're in the suburbs).

When any of this material is delivered, it pays to have a pathway cleared for the truck, so it can dump the load where you want it or as close as possible. A typical load that may cost less than a pair of shoes (in regular fill) may easily weigh from four to ten *tons*. So you won't want to carry it very far by hand.

Companies that make a business of selling and delivering this type of material usually have experienced drivers who can make your final hand-rakeout job a lot easier. For example, if you let the driver know as soon as he arrives just what area you plan to cover with the fill, he can often dump it in a series of small piles, spaced over the area, instead of one big one. This makes it much easier to spread. The best time to spread any type of earth is immediately after it's delivered, before it has a chance to pack. One of the best hand tools for spreading it is an ordinary iron rake. But you use the rake upside down (with prongs or tines up).

ESTIMATING THE AMOUNT FOR THE JOB

The unit of measure for all this material is the cubic yard. To estimate how many cubic yards of fill you need, think of the cubic yard in terms of slices. Each cubic yard will give you thirty-six slices 1 inch thick, or eighteen slices 2 inches thick, or nine slices 4 inches thick, and so on. Just measure the area you have to cover and decide how thick it must be (enough topsoil to cover exposed tree roots, for example), and the rest is easy. Each slice will be a yard square. Usually the smallest load you can buy at the regular price is three or four yards. If you buy less, it costs you more per yard.

If you have only a very small hollow to fill, such as a rainy-day puddle, your best bet may be a standard bag of mason's sand—but *don't* buy cement. You can buy this at most large lumberyards. Dig up some of the topsoil from the bottom of the puddle area, fill in with sand, and put the topsoil back on top. If there's good sod over the area, just lift it off, fill the area with the sand, and mix in some of the lower topsoil; then put the sod back, and water it well for a while.

THE PROS AND CONS OF VARIOUS PATIO MATERIALS

Most of these are easy for even a beginner to use. And they're economical if you know how to buy them. Crushed stone is one of the easiest to use, and usually the least expensive. If you plan to use a lawn area for a patio, it pays to shovel off at least a shallow layer of topsoil for two reasons. You can probably use the sod or topsoil somewhere else to improve your lawn (it would be wasted under the crushed stone), and removing it will reduce the chance of grass growing up through the stone. If you're lazy, however, just leave it there and soak the gravel with DuPont Ammate, which kills just about everything that grows. The right-sized crushed stone for a patio is ½ inch (the size screen it passes through), the same as for driveways. You figure the amount on the slice basis already described.

Cement patio blocks are one of the least expensive of the smooth surfaces you can use for a patio. These are usually 16 inches long, 8 inches wide, and 1 or 2 inches thick. They cost less in the natural cement color than in dyed types. You can lay them over ordinary ground or bed them in a layer of plain mason's sand. Either way you'll need a shovel and a garden trowel to skim the ground level here and there to keep the surface of the blocks even.

Brick is another attractive patio surface that can be laid in the same manner. A standard building brick is 8¼ inches long, 4 inches wide, and 2½ inches thick. You can lay them either flat or on edge in an almost limitless choice of patterns. Although they don't cost much new, many landscapers prefer the texture and color of old brick—which is available from building wreckers at about half the price of new brick. Locate the building wreckers near you in the yellow pages of your phone book, and make a few calls to find one who has a supply of used brick on hand.

Blacktop of the do-it-yourself variety covers 8 square feet of patio 1 inch thick per bag of average size. You rake it out and tamp it firm. You get a good, smooth surface, but it can get mighty hot if it's in a sunny area; and when it's hot, spike heels may sink in it. In a shady spot, however, it makes a very nice patio.

Flagstone, the old favorite, is in the higher price range. It costs most when it's cut in easy-to-use squares and rectangles, least when it's free-form. A little assortment of colors, of course, makes the surface more interesting. It can be laid over the earth or in sand. If you dream about a flagstone patio, it'll pay you to scout around the building wreckers' storage yards. This way you're likely to find what you need at around half the usual price.

Poured concrete gives you a patio you can dance on, and it's not as expensive as most people think. The best way to get it is in a ready-mix truck that dumps it down a chute wherever you want it—if the truck can reach the spot. A cubic yard typically costs about as much as a tire for the family car (a little more if you buy less than 3 yards in most areas). To confine it to the space you want to cover, you make a rim of 2 x 4s (on edge) and spread the concrete inside it. To prevent it from cracking when the earth under it heaves in winter, you use iron mesh made for the purpose. Just lay the mesh inside the rimmed space, held above the ground surface by small stones or lengths of wire. When the concrete is spread, the mesh will be inside of it. If you have ground-water problems, ask your concrete supplier for advice as to whether you need a layer of something else under the concrete. In any event, always tell the supplier what you are using the concrete for. Then you can be sure the truck will arrive with the right mix. When you make the rim for a concrete patio, be sure it's level. And plan it so you can slide a length of 2 x 4 along the top of the rim (with the ends of the sliding 2 x 4 on opposite sides of the rim) to screed it even. As most of us don't do many concrete jobs, it's usually a good idea to rent any special tools for it. The rental dealer will also give you the basic information on using them.

WHEN TO USE DRAINAGE TILES

Drainage tiles are also likely to figure in your outdoor handiwork. The ceramic and cement forms are usually made in 1-foot lengths. The ceramic ones look like red crockery and are harder and more expensive than the cement ones. But for ordinary lawn drainage, the cement variety is often the best budget bet. If you have a mushy spot on your lawn, as where a downspout from the rain gutter empties, you can distribute the outpouring with a few lengths of tile—aimed along the downslope of the lawn. You can do a fancy job by digging a shallow trench for the tiles and filling under them with some crushed stone. Leave about ⅜ inch between the tiles, cover the top of the space between them with tar paper, and fill the trench with crushed stone topped off with sod or topsoil. Let the final tile protrude from the slope if the run is short. But you can push some crushed stone into it so the water spreads instead of gushing. The same general principle can be followed in using tiles to drain a pocket in the lawn where rain water puddles.

WORKING WITH CEMENT

Small cement jobs are likely to be involved here and there in your outdoor fix-ups. For these, ready-mixed (dry) cement like Sacrete is your best bet. There are several methods of mixing in the water to make the stuff ready for use. In one, you just empty the bag of dry mix on a flat surface like a piece of plywood. It's a good idea to churn up the dry mix with a hoe to make sure all the ingredients are thoroughly mixed, as the heavy sand sometimes tends to settle to the bottom of the bag in shipping. After this little precaution, pile up the dry mix to form a little hill. Then hollow out the top of the hill to form a deep hollow like the crater in a volcano. You pour the water into this crater a little at a time, and pull the dry mix down from the sides gradually with a hoe, mixing it with the water as you go along. In the final stages you'll be pulling cement in from the outer rim of the little hill. This works fine if you're careful not to break through the rim of your little volcano before the mixing is complete. If you break through it, the water will run out and wash away some of your cement.

An easier mixing job can be done in either a metal garden cart or a metal wheelbarrow—if you happen to have either one in the usual small bathtublike form. Just dump the bag of dry cement mix into the metal body, add the required amount of water, and slosh it all together with a hoe.

However you mix your ready-type cement, you're likely to find the final product somewhat stiffer than you expect. That's because the amount of water specified on the bag is calculated to give the cement its highest strength in hardening. But the stiff mixture may not be easy to work into cracks or between stones, if you're doing that kind of work. So add a *little* more water. You have to do this in stingy fashion, not more than a cup at a time. The reason: after a certain amount of water is added to a cement-sand mix, a very small additional amount may turn it into a soupy slush very suddenly. The mixture is easiest to work with in crack and stone work when it's about the consistency of apple butter. When it's slushy you have a tough time making it stay put on anything, and it's weaker when it hardens.

HOW TO APPLY CEMENT MORTAR

If you're building something with stones or masonry blocks, try to get the kind of cement mix that's made specially for the purpose. It's usually labeled mortar mix. This has a little lime in it to make it stick to things when it's wet. This makes it much handier when you have to stick it to something vertical—like the vertical edges of cement blocks. You have to be much more careful with the regular mix because it tends to slough off. If you're working with cement blocks, aim to get an even spread of cement on the top of each one so the one on top will set evenly. And stand back and take a look at the whole thing frequently to see if you're getting it straight or skewed. It's a lot easier to correct errors while the cement's wet than after it hardens. And it begins hardening in about half an hour. For this reason you may want to mix only half a bag at a time until you get the knack.

The best way to work the cement into crevices, or to spread it on blocks, bricks, or stones is by troweling. You can buy a mason's trowel at hardware or dime stores. Unless you're planning to build a stone fortress, you can get along with a cheap one. You can make your work easier, however, by getting two—a little one and a big one. You can use the big one to bring the cement to the spot where you're working, and the little one to apply it, letting the big one serve as a supply tray. You can hold it close to the crevice you're filling and push the right amount of cement in with the little trowel. The pros use a wider variety of tools, but this works fine and costs less.

If you turn out to be a messy mason and are slopping cement all over the place with your trowel, don't be afraid to use your hands in childhood mud-pie style. As the cement isn't exactly a good hand lotion, however, it pays to wear an old pair of rubber gloves for this primitive technique. Simply scoop up blobs of cement in the sizes needed to fill in holes between stones, or to smear along the edges of masonry blocks, and do the job by plain, crude shove-and-smear methods. The end result is likely to look more professional than if you did it with the right tools.

When you get through with your cement work, wash whatever

tools you used and hose out the garden cart or wheelbarrow. Once the cement hardens, you have to bang it off of things, which isn't always easy.

RAIN GUTTERS AND DOWNSPOUTS

If these aren't causing trouble, leave them alone. If the gutters get clogged with leaves, you can buy wire strainers at the hardware store to fit into the openings from the gutter into the downspouts. Then the strainer gets clogged with leaves. Either way, you'll have to climb a ladder after the leaves have fallen in late autumn, and scoop the leaves out of the gutters.

You should use the strainers if you also use one of the roll-out plastic spray hoses at the bottom of your downspouts. These things fit on the lower end of the downspout, rolled up like a jelly roll. When it rains, they unroll like the Hallowe'en paper snakes you used to blow to unroll when you were a kid. The roll-out downspout hose, however, serves a more useful purpose. It has holes along it so the rain water sprays out in dozens of tiny fountains. This distributes the water flow over a large lawn area instead of shooting it all at one spot where it can cause a washout. But if you have a puppy, keep him inside when it rains. Otherwise he may be fascinated by the big snake unrolling on the lawn, and decide to bring it to the front door so you can see what he has captured. And remember, too, that your roll-out hoses must be detached and brought indoors for the winter.

HOW TO REPAIR CORRODED GUTTERS

If your gutters are galvanized and are showing signs of major rusting (usually inside the gutter, along the bottom), you can get quite a few more years of service out of them by painting them with asphalt roof paint. This stuff is black and tarry (but it's not tar), and it's one of the cheapest coatings you can buy. If you get it on your hands, you can take it off with kerosene or even cooking oil or cold cream, followed by detergent.

If the gutter has already rusted through and is dripping, you may still be able to get more years out of it. If the big trouble is confined to a relatively short section, it may pay to fix it. Buy a piece of aluminum flashing from the lumberyard, long enough to cover the necessary length of gutter. This flashing is thin aluminum in such soft form you can cut it with ordinary scissors. And it's very easy to shape to fit the inside of the gutter. Buy the narrowest width available and cut it narrower (it's usually too wide) so it just covers te inside of the gutter. Then coat the inside of the gutter where it is to go with asphalt roofing cement. This is a lot like the asphalt roof paint, but much thicker. And it's also cheap. Once you stick the aluminum down in this, it's there to stay—and your leak is cured. If you live close to a salt-water shore, however, this kind of repair won't last as long—if salt spray can reach it. The galvanic action between the two different metals results in further corrosion.

CARING FOR WOOD AND METAL GARDEN TOOLS

Garden tools will last a lot longer if you take a little care of them. And they'll work better if you keep them in good shape. If wooden handles lose their protective finish coat, sand them smooth. You don't have to sand off remaining finish that still adheres firmly—but if you enjoy sanding, go ahead. You can refinish them with a couple of coats of spar varnish. This goes over most similar finishes without fighting them, and it stands up beautifully if it's a good brand. (There are lots of good ones.) You use this stuff not only to make the tool last longer but to keep it smooth and easy on the hands. If you let wooden tool handles go to pot, weathering may raise a splinter here and there that you may eventually have to pull out of your fingers.

Painted metal parts don't require much attention. But if you make a habit of sanding and painting the little spots that occasionally show up rusty, your equipment is likely to last for the next hundred years. Do the touch-up as soon as you spot the rust. Just keep a couple of small cans of outdoor enamel around in colors that are somewhere near your tool colors. And keep a couple of small, cheap brushes in a jar with enough turpentine to cover the bristles. You can wrap some aluminum foil around the jar at the top to close it, even though the brush handles are sticking up inside the foil. This keeps the turpentine from evaporating too fast. If it goes down a little, add some more. You don't have to be fussy about any of this. The brushes may get a little raggy, but they'll do the job. And if the paint doesn't match perfectly, it still looks better than a hole with a rusty rim around it. If you end up with a blotchy-looking garden cart, you can always paint the whole thing some winter night when you have nothing better to do.

SHARPENING KNOW-HOW FOR GARDEN TOOLS

With some experience you can sharpen any garden tool. But without it, you'll do well to skip the garden shears as they can be ruined by energetic bungling. Just in case you decided to try it anyway, however, sharpen only the bevels—*not* the flat, meeting surfaces of the blades. And above all, do as little sharpening as possible. Because of technical details you can't easily see, each time you sharpen shears or scissors you remove a little metal from important areas, and bring the tools closer to the day when they refuse to cut.

One of the handiest sharpening tools you can have is a sharpening file for a power mower. Simonds is one of the file makers with a beauty in this line. (They're in Fitchburg, Massachusetts, in case you can't get this kind of file locally.) You don't use this tool on power mowers alone, but on assorted grass cutting, even some digging tools.

SHARPENING THE BLADE OF A ROTARY MOWER

Whether you're sharpening a power mower blade (rotary mower) or a grass whip—that wonderful odd-job tool that swings like a golf club—the principle is the same. Without removing the blade from the mower, look at the bevel on the cutting edge to get an idea of the correct angle, lay the file on the bevel, and start filing. This removes the bumps and batters close to the cutting edge. If there are nicks in the blade (little ones), you don't have to file the whole edge down to get rid of the nicks. Use a small round file (sometimes called a rattail file), to sharpen the nicks instead. If you find a really big nick in a power mower blade, or if you spot the slightest evidence of a crack, throw the blade away. New ones are cheaper than you may realize—and a lot cheaper than your bills might be if the blade flew apart and hit you. After you've filed off the bumps, you can tilt the file a little more steeply to sharpen the very edge of the blade. You'll hear all sorts of precision talk about rotary mower sharpening, but the important point is safety. Don't reuse a badly battered blade. (Your mower owner's manual tells you how to replace it.) The thing turns so fast that it cuts nicely if you do any kind of fairly decent sharpening job. It even cuts if it's completely dull—but it shreds the cut grass ends and makes your lawn look brownish when it should look green. If your owner's manual offers any specific sharpening information, by all means follow it. Some have gimmicks that make sharpening easier than usual. One very important point: *never*—repeat—*never* touch the blade of a power mower (any kind of power mower) unless the ignition wires are completely disconnected at the spark plug (or plugs.) Even if the motor is tipped over, the gas tank empty, there can be enough gas to let the motor kick over when you move the blade. And just one kick-over can put you in the hospital minus some fingers or worse. Mowermakers warn you about this. Don't let any smart aleck talk you out of caution.

TIPS FOR REEL MOWERS

One thing seldom mentioned about reel mowers is their ability to sharpen themselves to a considerable extent. The way the revolving blades scrape over the cutter bar actually tends to keep renewing the keen edge of both, rather than dulling it. So these things often go for years without much attention. If yours stops cutting and you have no mechanical sense, don't fool with it. Your hardware dealer can tell you where to get it sharpened or take care of it for you. If you have a mechanical turn of mind, however, take a look at the cutter bar. You'll see a couple of big screws at each end of it, and you'll see which one you should tighten to bring the bar closer to the revolving blades. Adjust these so the revolving blades make an audible scraping noise as they pass the bar. Then smear the bar (on its blade-contacting surface) with some valve-grinding abrasive paste (automotive suppliers carry it), and give the revolving blades a dozen or more turns backward. Then feel the cutting corners of the blades and the bar. Usually they'll feel a lot keener than before. Then wash off all the abrasive with water and detergent, and adjust the cutter bar. The revolving blades should make just a whispering sound as they pass it. (They shouldn't miss it altogether—just pass it with a kiss.) With this behind you, the chances are your mower will work like new.

A few final tips. Before you decide to tackle a major sharpening job on a reel mower, try simply readjusting those cutter bar screws to get that whisper contact in passing. Often one side of the mower cuts grass just fine while the other side leaves tufts sticking up after you've gone by. This simply means that the tufty side of the cutter bar needs to be adjusted a trifle closer to the revolving blades. You don't need any valve-grinding compound. A big screwdriver can do the trick. There are plenty of old reel mowers around, doing a magnificent job without having been really sharpened for close to a generation. If yours is acting up, play around with the adjustments, using a delicate, intellectual touch. Your efforts will almost always be crowned with success.

SHOVELS

Shovels need sharpening, too. Most of them aren't sharpened when you buy them, but they make your digging easier if they are. Use a half-round file (from the hardware store) about 10 inches long with a bastard cut. Sharpen the inner edge of the shovel with the rounded side of the file, and do it as evenly as possible. You'll find your shovel enters the earth much more easily and shears through roots that are in the way.

If you aren't familiar with shovels, this is a good time to size them up. For digging good-sized holes, your best bet is a long-handled shovel with the handle almost parallel to the blade. This lets you stand on the upper edge of the blade to shove it into the ground without reaching way out in front to grip the handle. If you want to shovel things up from the ground or from the garage floor, you want a long-handled shovel with the blade tipped up at an angle in relation to the handle. This lets you slide the blade along the floor without bending way down to grip the handle. The difference in these two shovel styles makes the difference between comfortable work and an aching back. You can single out the right one in the hardware store by laying the blade flat on the floor and noting the position of the handle. Major manufacturers turn out a number of variations from one extreme to the other.

If you have to throw with the shovel to land stuff some distance away with accuracy (the way boiler room coal shovelers do it), you want a D-handled shovel. You can spot this easily as the handle has a distinct D-shape that lets you tip the blade with full control.

WHEN TO USE A SPADE

The spade is essentially a shovel with a squared entering edge. This comes in handy for jobs like transplanting because the square edge shears through roots that a pointed shovel would push aside. Also the spade makes a trench with a flat bottom—handy in many types of work. But it doesn't penetrate as easily so it's not as good for the big-digging, tiring jobs. Like the shovel, it should be sharpened.

13

HOW TO FIX A CAR WITHOUT KNOWING HOW

If you rely on a car at all you probably can't get along without it even for a little while. When something goes wrong with it you miss trains, run out of food, leave people stranded on street corners, or spend the night stalled on some lonesome road out in nowhere. Yet most of the troubles that immobilize you are the kind you can fix if you know how. At least, you can usually fix them well enough to get you to a mechanic who can fix them—and the chances are you'll get where you were headed, without being stranded.

You can learn most of what you need to know by simply sticking around for a while the next time your car gets its periodic servicing. Watch what goes on and ask the service man to show you some of the things you may have to work on if you ever get stuck. You'll see why in the next few pages. You want to know how to get the carburetor air cleaner off, where the fuel line is, where the spark plugs and distributor are, and how to get the radiator cap off. All this in case you're one of the growing multitude who drive a car without knowing anything whatever about how it works. (Housewives are often in this category even though the man of the house is an omniscient automotive nut.)

WHEN THE CAR WON'T START

When the car won't start in the morning, the *way* it fails to start is your first clue to the kind of ailment it has. If you turn the ignition key and go through the usual starting procedure and find that absolutely nothing happens—no sound, no starter, no nothing—you have the most frustrating ailment of all, a dead battery. So we'll tackle that first.

PUTTING LIFE INTO A DEAD BATTERY

If you have a standard transmission (not automatic), you can have somebody push you with another car to get you started, but this isn't likely. The other fellow probably won't want to risk damaging his automatic transmission. If he also has a standard transmission, however, here's how it's done: assuming your car is where your rescuer can ease up behind it bumper to bumper, and push you along the road, pump the gas pedal a few times, set your shift lever in high and push your clutch out (disengaged). Have your ignition turned on. When your car reaches about 15 miles an hour, ease the clutch in gently so the motor turns over. Usually it will start after a short clutch-in run. Then disengage the clutch and let the motor warm up for a couple of minutes while you sit still with your foot on the gas pedal. But *do not* race the motor. Just keep it running at moderate speed so it won't stall. And when you drive away, shift gently and don't stall the motor. After it has run for a while the generator or alternator will put a charge in the battery—if the battery is any good. Have the battery checked at a good service station.

If you and all your possible rescuers have automatic transmissions, it's still possible to get a push-start, but unless you and your rescuer know just what to do, you can end up with transmission damage. If you both have an owner's manual, you'll find the answers easily. Otherwise, skip the push start.

Another way to start a car with a dead battery is by means of battery booster or jumper cables. These are just long insulated cables with spring clamps on both ends. You just connect them from the battery in somebody else's car to the battery in yours so you can use the other fellow's battery to start your car. You can carry these things in your luggage compartment in case you need them. The important thing is to connect the "plus" terminal of the other fellow's battery to the "plus" terminal of your battery, and do the same with the "minus" terminals. Car batteries are marked to show which is which. When you buy the cables, get the salesman to show you how to find the battery markings. And be sure that your car and the other fellow's car have the same battery voltage—either 12 volts or 6 volts. When you use these things, you just hook them up from one car to the other and then start the motor in the usual way.

Loose battery connections can sometimes create the same effect as a dead battery. To find out if they're loose, try to wiggle them with your hands. If one of them wiggles and you have pliers in your glove compartment, use the pliers to tighten the nut that squeezes the cable clamp on the battery connecting post. If you have no pliers and you're stuck in the wilds, you can sometimes get a better electrical contact by forcing the end of a safety pin (or other sharp pin) down between the clamp and the battery connecting post. Several ordinary straight pins have often done the trick.

THE STARTER SPINS, BUT THE MOTOR FAILS TO START

If the starter spins the motor but the motor won't start, your sense of smell may lead you to the trouble. If, with the hood up, you smell gasoline, your automatic choke may be stuck. To find out, you take off the air cleaner—usually a big thing on top of the motor that looks like a chicken fryer. The choke valve is a flat thing in the carburetor opening under the air cleaner. It looks a lot like an old-fashioned chimney damper. Poke its lower side downward with your finger tip. If it's hard to poke open, it's undoubtedly the troublemaker. These things sometimes get jammed shut by a backfire that you may not even hear. If you have somebody with you, have him hold the choke open with a stick (so a possible backfire won't singe his hand) while you try starting the motor again. It'll have to spin over a number of times to clear out the flooded gas that accumulated when it was stuck. Once it starts, your friend can pull his stick out. Let the motor warm up. When it's warm, the choke should remain open. If it doesn't, there's something wrong with it. Use a piece of string or wire (as from a paper clip or bobby pin) to hold the outside choke lever arm so the choke valve stays open. And get the thing fixed before you have to start the motor again. Once you get the motor running the first time, you can put the air cleaner back. But if it's hard to put back with the engine running, leave it off until you get to a service station. Just park the thing in the trunk.

HUMIDITY CAN AFFECT STARTING

On very humid mornings, winter or summer, your motor may kick and cough as the starter turns it over, but it may not start. The trouble can often be cured with a handkerchief or a facial tissue. First, wipe off the white porcelain parts of the spark plugs. Then slide the cloth or tissue along the fat insulated wires from the spark plugs to the distributor to wipe away any moisture on them. And do the same thing with the fat wire that leads from the center of the distributor to the spark coil. Once all this is done (it seldom takes more than a minute or two), try starting the motor again. The motor usually starts after this treatment (unless it's a wreck anyway), but it may run weakly and unevenly. Just keep it running at moderate speed while the car sits still for a few minutes. As the motor warms up, the heat will dry up the moisture that's making it run so badly, and before long it will smooth out. New ignition leads (those fat insulated wires) often cure this trouble. Talk to your mechanic about it.

One thing you *should not* do in the course of your motor nursing is tramp the gas pedal. Don't push it down, then let it up so you get that vroom-vroom-vroom sound effect. This is kid stuff. It ruins the air-gas mixture and, more often than not, stalls the motor. And it can't possibly do any good.

WHAT TO DO FOR A VAPOR LOCK

If the motor quits while you're driving, the *way* it quits may tell you something important. If it slows down gradually as though you had eased your foot off the gas pedal, you may be out of gas. Gas gauges often go haywire and tell you the tank is full when it isn't. With the ignition off, try pumping the gas pedal. Then try the starter. If the motor doesn't start, or if it runs for a few seconds, then quits again, you're probably not getting gas at the motor. In very hot weather this can be caused by a vapor lock even when you have plenty of gas. This results from gasoline actually boiling in the fuel line where it passes something very hot, like the exhaust manifold. The boiling creates a big bubble in the fuel line so the fuel pump can't suck gas through to the motor. To cure the trouble, shut off the motor, open the hood, and let it all cool off. If you can get a teakettle of cold water from a nearby house, you can pour it *carefully* over the fuel line at the point that comes closest to the hot motor. But don't let any water splash on a hot exhaust manifold, as this might crack it. You can spot the manifold in most cases because it's the biggest thing that looks rusty on the side of the motor.

COLD WEATHER STARTING TIPS

In cold weather your motor may quit in much the same fashion because your fuel line is frozen. Little droplets of water that get into your gas tank from condensation or rain build up into an ice blockage, usually at some very low point in the fuel line. In a really serious pickle you can often thaw it with hot antifreeze from the radiator. Push a cloth or handkerchief (*never* a paper facial tissue) into the radiator fluid after removing the radiator cap. Then, while the antifreeze is still hot, slap it on the lowest point of the fuel line that you can reach. The heat spreads along the line. If you can get a teakettle of hot water from a nearby house, pour hot water on the line slowly to let the heat spread as far as possible. Then try to start the motor. If it starts, get to a gas station as quickly as you can and buy one of the anti-icing additives like Dry-Gas. These mix with any water that happens to be in the gas tank, and prevent it from freezing.

THAWING FROZEN DOOR BUTTONS AND LOCKS

If the door lock is frozen on a cold night so that you can't even unlock the door, your best bet is a wind-proof lighter like a

Zippo, or a pack of matches. As most of today's car locks are mounted in the door itself, you can't heat them directly. So you put on your gloves and heat the business end of the key—the part that goes into the lock. Then put the key in the lock and turn it gently in the direction that should unlock the door. This brings the heated key in firm contact with the frozen lock parts. On bitter cold nights you may have to do this three or four times, but it usually works.

If the door-opening button is frozen so you can't push it in to open the door, hold the lighter or match flame under it. Usually, in around ten seconds, enough heat is conducted along the button to free it. Then you can open the door. If the whole business is covered with sleet, crack the sleet off with light taps of a pocket-knife or whatever you happen to have, before you apply the flame.

14

THE NOT-SO-AWFUL HANDYMAN

ONCE we collect a little batch of tools, not many of us are content to go through life merely fixing things. We start putting up shelves, hanging pictures and mirrors, and we usually wind up by actually building things. After we get that far, there's really no limit. People who never did anything like it before have built just about everything from bookcases to yachts and airplanes, and they've done it beautifully.

Buying the materials, is, of course, the first step in making something. And, as most of us use more wood than metal in the things we make, the lumberyard is a good place to start. In fact, when you know the ins and outs of lumber you can buy it in forms that eliminate a large part of the work you have to do.

HOW TO FIGURE THE COST OF LUMBER

The board foot is the measuring unit by which you buy most lumber. This is simply a piece of lumber 1 foot square and 1 inch, or less, thick. If you buy a board 10 feet long, 1 foot wide, and 1 inch thick you have bought 10 board feet. If it's thinner than 1 inch thick, it's 10 board feet anyway. If the board is only 6 inches wide but 10 feet long, it's 5 board feet. Whatever the width, you just add up the total area and figure it in board feet. If the board is 2 inches thick—say, 10 feet long, a foot wide, and two inches thick—you have 20 board feet. So if you know the price per board foot, you can use simple arithmetic to figure the cost of any width, thickness, or length.

WHAT NOMINAL SIZES ARE

There's one point that baffles some beginners. Standard lumber sizes are nominal sizes. They're not quite as thick or as wide as their nominal size implies. A 1 x 12 (meaning 1 inch thick and 12 inches wide), for example, is really only 25/32 inch thick and 11½ inches wide. But you're not being gypped. The lumber was full-sized when it came from the saw at the mill, but some of it was shaved off in smoothing it, and it shrank a little as it dried out in seasoning. So when you want a board that's really 1 inch thick (instead of a nominal inch) you ask for full inch. (It costs more.) As most woodworking is based on the nominal sizes, however, you won't need the full-inch size very often.

LUMBER GRADES AND HOW TO SELECT THEM

The board foot price of lumber varies with the *kind* of wood and the quality. Most hardwoods (like oak) cost more than soft ones (like pine). And, in general, wood with flaws in it, like knotholes, costs less than wood that's unblemished. The established methods of grading lumber vary somewhat with the different woods. And modern efforts to simplify it to the moron level have made the whole business somewhat confusing. But in general, the pine that you're most likely to use for projects is still classed this way; the top grade is called 1 and 2 clear, B and better, or firsts and seconds. All three terms mean top grade. If you simply ask for *clear* pine you'll usually get the prime quality. This is really pretty wood, with no knots or flaws. It takes a beautiful finish, but it's also at the top of the price list. So don't pick this grade for shelves on the cellar wall. You might as well buy filet mignon to make hash.

The next two lower grades are C-select and D-select, each with minor flaws, but both suited to natural finishing. Below these two are the board grades from 1 to 5 (though many lumberyards don't stock the lowest grades), with progressively greater flaws. The number 1 board grade, however, is usually a good all-round quality, especially for making things that will be painted. And if you poke around the lumber pile, you're also likely to find pieces of it (a board here and there) perfectly suitable for natural finishing. The explanation: lumber is graded at the mill by eye, so you're likely to find a few pieces a little better or worse in any grade. If your lumber dealer is a good-natured soul, he may not

To use board grade lumber for natural finish work, cut out the sections that contain flaws, as shown by the dotted lines. If your project doesn't require long pieces, you can cut costs this way.

mind your bargain-hunting. But don't mix up the lumber stacks.

For strictly utility jobs, you can use still lower grades. The strength of the lumber doesn't diminish much till you reach the bottom of the grading scale. But you may have to contend with a few splits, stains, and knotholes. For many projects, however, you can do as the industrial customers do. Use the clear lumber between the flaws in a board. If the parts of your project aren't too long, this is an easy way to save money. Just cut the board so the pieces you use don't have flaws in them.

WHAT LUMBER TERMS MEAN

Tongues, grooves, and square edges are some of the standard lumber features you'll encounter. The edges of the hardwood-finish flooring in your house are tongued and grooved. The tongue along the edge of one flooring strip fits into a groove along the edge of the next one so the whole floor ties together like a big sheet of wood. The same kind of edges are used on the lower quality boards under the flooring (called the subfloor) and on the planking under the outside covering of your house. Although plywood is taking the place of these tongue-and-groove boards (abbreviated T&G) for many purposes, they're still around in great quantity, and are usually low-priced. But they're not very well suited to most household projects, like shelves or built-ins. The handiest lumber for shelves is square-edged in whatever width you want. (Widths usually run from 1 x 2 to 1 x 12 in 2-inch steps, 1 x 4, 1 x 6, etc.) Lengths usually run from 4 feet to around 16 feet in 2-foot steps. But many lumberyards will cut you a 2-foot piece if you need it, as it simply reduces the remaining piece to the next shorter standard size. If you order your lumber in the lengths you'll be using (where possible), you can save yourself most of the sawing work. For although the width and thickness of nominal-size lumber is always a little under, the length should be full-length.

WHEN TO USE HEAVIER LUMBER

Heavier lumber like 2 x 4s and 2 x 6s also comes in handy on many jobs that require considerable strength. You might use it, for example, to make the framework of a playhouse, or perhaps a garden bridge. The 2 x 4s are also good for patio railings. In most areas this heavier lumber is fir rather than pine. It's darker in color, harder, and stronger. And some people think it's not as pretty as pine. But properly stained and finished, it makes very attractive outdoor furniture.

PLYWOOD GRADES FOR ALL TYPES OF WORK

Plywood is great stuff for projects that involve large areas, like kitchen cabinets and Ping-pong tables. Most of it comes in 4-foot by 8-foot panels. At most lumberyards the thicknesses available range from ¼ inch up to ¾ inch in ⅛-inch steps, but intermediate thicknesses and greater maximum thickness is stocked by some of the big outlets. The least expensive plywood has a fir outer veneer on both surfaces. The surfaces are graded by letters according to their freedom from flaws. A near-perfect surface, for example, is graded A. A surface with veneer patches and certain other flaws like knots, is graded C. For any job where only one side will show, your best bet is what is called A-C plywood. This is a very popular grade with a near-perfect surface on one side (the side that will show) and some unimportant flaws on the other—reducing the price considerably. This is your best bet for things like kitchen cabinets.

If you want to finish plywood in the natural wood, you can get it with an outer veneer of almost any species of wood the world has ever known, from cocobolo to walnut or teak. But you'll have to order it in advance, and you'd better be sure to find out the price in advance. A few of them may make your hair stand up. But popular decorative woods of the mahogany family are often surprisingly reasonable, as are a number of other attractive but plentiful varieties. You can also buy your plywood with plastic laminate on it (at some outlets) and with special resin-impregnated surfaces that take a supersmooth finish with no grain showing through a painted surface.

If you are making something to be used out of doors (like a doghouse or a patio table), be *sure* you buy exterior-grade plywood. This is made with completely waterproof glue between the layers. If you try to save a few cents by using interior grade, the veneers are likely to separate over a period of time.

If your project calls for a long run of narrow widths of plywood, like counter tops, ask your lumberyard about counter-top sizes. These are stocked by many yards, and can save you a lot of sawing and sometimes a lot of money.

FANCY PRESHAPED LUMBER DRESSES UP HOME PROJECTS

Fancy things stocked by lumberyards are increasing in number so fast that only frequent visits can keep you up to date. But some of the established items are worth knowing about. You can get wooden moldings, for example, in all sorts of shapes and sizes. Used to trim plain, square-edged lumber, this molding can make the difference between something that looks like an old crate and something that might be a Chippendale creation. You'll find the moldings stored in racks at the lumberyard. Spend a little time looking at them. Then decide how you can make use of them. If your lumber dealer won't let you browse around the molding racks, look for a dealer who will. Remember that amateur home improvement work is a multibillion dollar annual business. So most lumberyards like you—if you're not a pest.

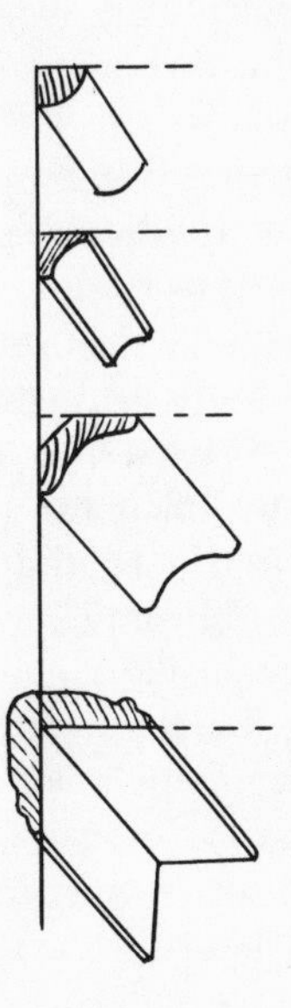

Four of dozens of ready-made moldings available from lumberyards. Left to right, quarter round (made in various sizes), cove molding, linoleum cove, corner bead, or outside corner molding. Check lumberyard molding racks for a type to suit your need.

FASTENINGS FOR EVERY PURPOSE

The term "fastenings" applies to all the things you'll be using to hold parts together. It covers nails, screws, bolts, and just about everything else except glue. There are so many types that it would take a book a lot bigger than this just to describe them all. But, fortunately, the ones you're most likely to use aren't quite so numerous.

TYPES OF NAILS AND HOW TO SELECT THEM

The common nail is the most familiar type. It has a point on one end and a flat, disk-shaped head on the other. This is the kind you use for the utility jobs like basement shelves and doghouses. It's a tough nail you can drive without too much worry about bending it, and it has pretty good holding power. But its head is conspicuous, so you don't pick this variety for the fancy jobs. The finishing nail is the one you use on the fancy jobs. It's skinnier than the common nail, and its head is much smaller and sort of knob-shaped so you can sink it below the wood surface by hammering it in with a nail set. Then you cover over it with wood filler, and nobody spots the nails after you do your finishing job.

Both types are sold traditionally by the "penny" size system. According to the most widely accepted explanation, this system originated with the number of pennies you'd have to pay (in the old days) for a hundred nails of each particular size. Thus, a little nail only 1½ inches long is a 4-penny nail because you could get a hundred of them for 4 cents. But a 6-inch nail is a 60-penny nail because it would cost you 60 cents to get a hundred. All this is fun if you like it, but you're much less likely to end up with the wrong size if you simply buy your nails according to their length. Ask for a 2-inch nail and you'll get it.

The simplest rule of the thumb for picking the correct length for the job is this: use a nail three times as long as the thickness of the board you're going to drive it *through*. Thus, if you're nailing an inch-thick board to something, you should use a 3-inch nail. The possible exception here occurs if a nail of that length will poke through the other side of the work and stick out where it shouldn't be. In this case, you can bend the poked-out end over to clinch it—if the appearance of the bent-over nail doesn't matter. If everything has to look nice, you can use a shorter nail. In any event, you should drive the nail through the thinner piece of wood into the thicker piece, and use as much length as you can to get the best holding power—up to three times the thickness of the thinner piece.

Form nails are another type that come in handy for a number of purposes. These look like common nails with two heads—one above the other. When you drive them into a piece of wood, the lower head seats firmly on the wood and leaves the upper head well above the surface. This lets you nail something together tightly while leaving one nail head (the upper one) above the surface so you can pull it out easily with a claw hammer. As the name implies, these nails are used on forms for such things as concrete walls and foundations. They hold everything together solidly until the concrete hardens, then they're easy to pull out so the wooden forms can be reused for the next concrete job. You'll often find them handy, too, for odd jobs where you want to leave a nail head sticking out to hang something on—like a heavy mirror.

Another type of nail that does special jobs is the screw nail. This takes many forms but all have spiral fluting on them. When you drive one of these nails, it turns as it goes into the wood. So it

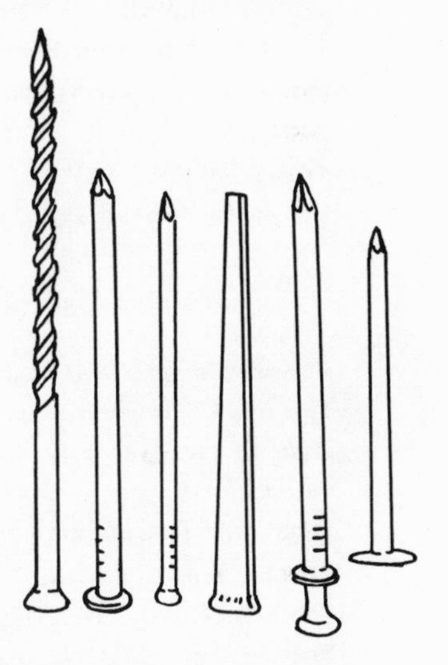

Nails you may use. (1), a screw nail; (2), a common nail for general rough work where nails aren't concealed; (3), a finishing nail that has a small head for driving slightly below surface for concealing with filler; (4) is a flooring cut nail. This is a special-purpose type that minimizes splitting. Two-header (5) is a form nail. The lower head seats on wood. The upper one stays above the surface for easy pulling later. (6), a big-headed galvanized roofing nail.

has to turn to come out of the wood. This increases the power required to pull it out, so it has greater holding power than an ordinary nail. It comes in handy where you need an especially firm grip, as in tightening down squeaky flooring.

There are also fetter ring nails with sharp ridges around them to get a screwlike grip when they're driven in. These are used for much the same purpose as the screw nails, but usually for special applications like boat-building. And for this use, you can get them in stainless steel.

You can also buy common nails made of aluminum for exterior

uses on your house or elsewhere. You have to drive them a little more carefully so as not to bend them, but they hold as well as the standard ones, and they never rust or make rust stains on the paint.

Flooring nails are another type you'll eventually see, and you may wonder why anybody would use them. These aren't round in their most familiar form, but flat. They have a crude, primitive look that makes you think they'd split anything they were driven into. But oddly, they have much less tendency to split the wood than ordinary nails. The reason: their points are squared off blunt. They shear their way through the wood instead of spreading the fibers apart with a sharp point. You won't be using these for actual flooring work as it takes a lot of experience to drive them at an angle through the edges of flooring strips the way the pros do it. But if you're interested in making imitation antiques, you may use a few flooring nails here and there because they resemble the nails of days gone by.

WHEN TO USE ROUND HEAD SCREWS AND FLATHEADS

Screws for wood-fastening come in a variety of basic forms, but the most commonly used ones are the *flat head, round head, and oval head.* The length of each type is measured according to the portion of the screw that actually goes into the wood. The diameter is specified by number, starting with number 1 for the smallest and ending with number 18 for the largest diameter generally available. So in typical lengths you have a wide choice from skinny screws to fat ones. If the screw has to go into the edge of a thin piece of wood, you pick a skinny one. One rule of the thumb tells you not to use a screw fatter than one fourth the thickness of a board if it is to be driven into the edge of the board.

There are various rules for selecting the length of a screw. But plain common sense is as good a guide as any. For one thing, you don't want a screw so long it goes all the way through the two parts being fastened and then sticks out the far side. And, of course, you don't want it so short its threaded portion cannot get a good hold. So you pick a screw with an unthreaded (smooth) shank just long enough to reach through the top board—so all of the threaded part goes into the bottom board—assuming you're driving the screw from the top. And you pick the diameter as

Screws are measured according to the length that actually goes into the wood. So round head screws are measured from the underside of the head to the point, flathead screws from the upper (flat) surface of the head to the point.

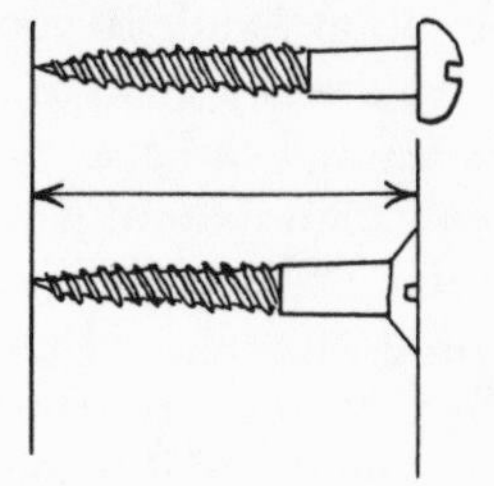

outlined earlier. If you're in doubt about the correct diameter, favor a screw on the skinny side and you won't have splitting problems.

COUNTERSINKING SCREWS AND CONCEALING HOLES

If the screw is being driven near the end or edge of a piece of wood, you should bore a pilot hole for it. This is a hole somewhat smaller than the screw diameter. It's intended to prevent splitting without spoiling the screw's grip in the wood. You have to make this kind of hole for a screw in hardwood whether it's near the end or edge or not. Otherwise you may break the screw trying to drive it in. There are many long lists of screw sizes and diameters, with drill sizes and diameters that correspond. But your best bet in drilling holes for screws is a little drill bit made especially for the purpose. Stanley makes these things under the name Screwmate. They come in little sets to match the common screw sizes and they don't cost much. They're especially handy when you're using flathead screws that require the usual countersunk recess to bring the head flush with the wood surface. The Screwmate bits for flathead screws not only make a hole of exactly the right diameter and depth for the smooth shank of the screw and for the threaded portion, but they also make the countersunk recess for the head. And they do the whole job in one shot. You don't bore separate holes. The drill bit has two different diameters, one for each section of the screw, plus an upper portion that does the countersinking. And everything matches the size and length of the screw.

As to which type of screw head to use, you simply match it to the job at hand. If you want to have a smooth surface, you use flathead screws. If the surface is going to be painted, you can let the screw head seat flush with the surface, and paint over it. If you want a natural wood finish, you can buy a special Screwmate bit that drills all the different diameter holes for the screw and the countersinking, and also a shallow hole as big as the head. Then you drive the screw head *below* the wood surface and glue a little wood plug into the hole above it. When you sand this smooth, the screw is hidden and all you see is wood. You can buy the wood plugs to match the bit sizes. Most fair-sized hardware stores (and many lumberyards) stock them in several different types of wood. They need not necessarily match the kind of wood you're using, as contrasting plugs create an attractive effect.

Use round head screws on things that you may want to take apart at some later date. For example, round heads are often used to fasten hi-fi units and speakers into cabinets so they can be removed for repairs or changes. Round heads are also the type to use when you fasten sheet metal to wood. (Flatheads would pull through if the thin metal was countersunk.)

The oval head screw is a sort of compromise between a flathead and a round head. It's head isn't flat, but just slightly convex. This is a good type to use where countersinking is possible (as for a flathead) but where you may want to remove the screws for one reason or another, as in hi-fi work. The slightly convex head can be removed easily without much risk of screwdriver damage to the wood surface. And you can get this type of screw with a polished brass or chrome finish on the head.

If you wonder when to use screws and when to use nails, think of it this way. Screws have much more holding power than most nails, so they're your best bet where there's a heavy load on the joined parts. And, often very important, you can drive a screw with almost no noise at all if you have to work at night when small fry are sleeping. Too, if delicate elements are involved, like radio, hi-fi, or TV, you'll be much wiser to use screws because no hammer impacts (which might damage frail parts) are required.

WHERE AND HOW TO USE TOGGLES, MOLLIES, AND MASONRY FASTENERS

Toggles, Mollies, and masonry fasteners are some of the things you can use to hold things together when ordinary nails or screws can't do the job. You can buy them in any hardware store.

The toggle bolt is one of the oldest and simplest. It's just a long, skinny bolt with a *folding* nut on it. If you want to fasten something to the inside wall of your house, and that something is fairly heavy, this is the kind of bolt for the job. First, you drill a

When you have to fasten something to a surface without being able to reach the other side to attach a nut to the bolt, you use either a toggle bolt or Molly bolt. The Molly, shown at top, starts out as a slit tube with a bolt inside. As the bolt is tightened, the slit tube buckles outward and seats its knees against the inside of the surface. The toggle bolt nut folds to pass through hole, as shown in the upper of the two lower drawings. Then it unfolds, as at bottom, to lock against the inside of the wall when the bolt is tightened.

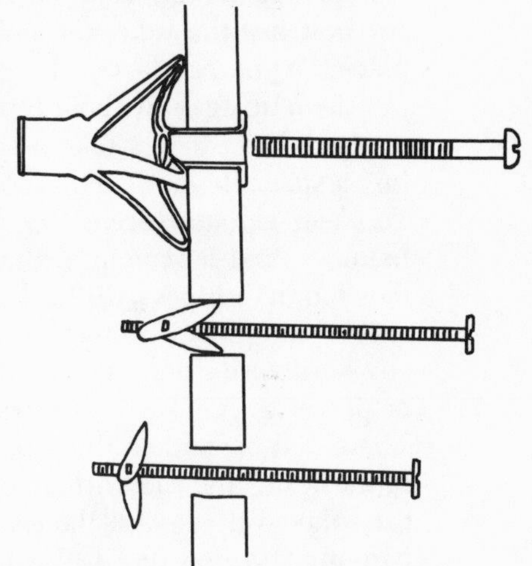

hole the size of the toggle bolt through the thing you want to fasten to the wall. Then you shove the toggle bolt through the hole with the head seated on the side toward you. Then you bore a hole through the plaster or wallboard just big enough to pass the folding nut in its folded position. Put the nut on the bolt (near the tip), fold it, and push it through the hole in the wall. As soon as the nut passes through the plaster, it unfolds inside the wall.

Now if you tighten the bolt, the nut draws up snug against the inside of the plaster or wallboard, and the job's done. If you want to remove the thing you've fastened to the wall, you just unscrew the bolt. The toggle's folding head falls off inside the wall, and you can pull the bolt out. To remount whatever you fastened to the wall, you simply use a new toggle bolt and nut. (You can't usually buy the folding nuts separately.)

The Molly bolt does the same job but in a different way. This one consists of an ordinary bolt inside of a thin metal tube with lengthwise slits in it. You bore a hole in the wall big enough to take the tube. Then you push the tube in the hole until a little flange on the screw-head end seats against the wall surface. Now if you tighten the bolt (it fits a nut on the other end of the tube), the slit portion of the tube buckles outward inside the wall and clamps against the inside of the wall. After this, you can remove the bolt but the tube, the nut, and the flange all stay solidly in place. So you can fasten things to the wall, take them down, and put them up again without replacing the Molly bolt.

Masonry fasteners take assorted forms. You can, for example, buy a specially hardened type that looks like a stubby screw nail. You can actually drive this thing into a cement block with a hammer, and it stays put. But it takes a little knack. One of the most popular types calls for boring a hole in the cement first. This isn't as tough as it sounds, as you can buy a masonry drill bit in any hardware store. You can use the bit in a hand drill, bit brace, or power drill. The power drill, of course, makes the job easiest. There's also another thing called a star drill. This looks like a black hexagonal rod with a splayed-out tip on one end. You hold the splayed tip against the cement and bang the other end with a hammer, turning the drill a little each time you bang it. All of these things make holes in cement faster than most amateurs expect. After you have the hole, you're ready for the fastener. In small holes you can use a fiber Rawlplug. This is a little fiber tube, often with a lead lining. You just shove it in the hole and drive a screw into the small hole down its center. As the screw goes in, it expands the Rawlplug against the interior of the hole and gets a mighty grip. For bigger holes and heavy loads there are various expansion bolts. Some of them have thick lead tubes that expand, others have hard-toothed shells. Happily, most of the established varieties work well. You'll be using things like this if you ever have to fasten something directly to your cellar wall.

ABOUT WOOD GLUES

If your fix-it job calls for gluing wood together or for gluing wood to something else, buy the right glue for the job. Some of today's everyday glues, originally developed to hold torpedo boats together, are so strong and so waterproof you can't weaken the joints they make even by boiling them for days. Other types will stick anything to anything, a patch on your overalls, for example, or a towel rack on a tile wall. And, of course, some glues cost more than others. The best rule: pick the cheapest glue that will do your particular job right. The trouble is that when you ask somebody which glue to use, he's likely to tell you the wrong one—as even hardware clerks may not always be too sure about which one is best for what. So here's a general guide to help you out:

Acrylic resin glue, like 3-Ton Adhesive, comes in two parts, a liquid and a powder. Mix as much as you need and it hardens in about five minutes at normal room temperature to a strength of around 3 tons per square inch. It sticks to almost anything, and has even been used to repair cracked diesel engine crankcases. It's one of the toughest of wood glues, and actually holds better in a fairly wide crack than a thin one. So it's tops as a gap-filler glue when you can't get your wood joints to fit snugly. But it's in the high price range. It smells like the stuff dentists often use to make white filling in your teeth, because it's practically the same stuff. Use it where you need an absolutely waterproof joint with the most of everything.

Aliphatic resin glue, like Titebond, is one of the newest furniture glue types. It's not waterpoof, but it's moisture-resistant, stronger than wood, and a good gap-filler type. It also has exceptional tack or stickiness that holds light parts together without clamping. On bigger jobs you need clamps for about forty-five minutes. This is a great medium-priced glue, ready-mixed, for furniture fixing. You can use it at temperatures down to 50 degrees.

Casein glue, like Elmer's Casein Glue, is a good old woodworking type in the low price range. It's a powder you mix with water just before you're ready to use it. It's not waterproof, but it's so water-resistant that it's still holding some European covered bridges together after better than a quarter century. Pick this one for big tough wood-gluing jobs especially in cold places —as it works fine at any weather temperature above freezing.

Cellulose nitrate cement, like Ever Fast, Duco Cement, and the other household tube varieties, is ready to use and a good choice for small wood-gluing jobs and repairs on other porous materials. It dries too fast for big jobs, as one end of the glue-coated area would be dry before you could finish the other end. After twenty-four hours of setting time, it's stronger than most people realize, with a breaking strength of about 1¾ ton per square inch of glued surface. And it starts holding after a few minutes. It isn't truly waterproof, though water only weakens its grip but doesn't dissolve it. It's a good glue for quick little fix-its like replacing loose furniture molding or putting broken bric-a-brac back together. It works on china and crockery that need not withstand frequent washing, and it holds metal to wood if you can use it so as to form a thin shell around the metal. Best way to use it on porous material: let the first coat dry for a few minutes on *both* surfaces to be joined, then apply a second coat to one surface and press the parts together. In the amounts likely to be used, you can figure this adhesive in the medium price range. A final caution: when you glue anything together with this or any other cement that smells like nail polish, don't leave it on a table top or other finished surface until it has dried for several days. The solvent may otherwise lift the finish.

Contact cement, made by scores of manufacturers, is a thin, syrupy, ready-to-use mix that usually contains synthetics like neoprene in toluol or naphtha. So it shouldn't be used around any open flame, including the pilot light on your kitchen range—if you cook with gas. And don't smoke when you use it. If you can't turn off the pilot light or you can't stop smoking, you can use a slightly higher-priced form that won't burn. The usual type that calls for fire precautions costs about as much as high quality paint.

This cement is different from the usual glues in that it is designed for the specific job of sticking fairly large areas of sheet materials to base surfaces, usually plywood. To do the job, you coat both surfaces to be joined (usually by brushing) and then let them dry for half to three quarters of an hour. Then cover the base surface with heavy wrapping paper. It won't stick to the surface if the cement is dry. Next, lay the other coated material (such as a sheet of plastic laminate for a counter top) on top of the wrapping paper and slide it around until it's lined up perfectly with the area it is to cover. To complete the job, have somebody hold the laminate sheet in position while you pull the wrapping paper out from between the two cement-coated surfaces. As soon as the two surfaces meet, they're stuck together for good. Use the heel of your hand or a rubber roller to press the two surfaces together, working outward from the center so as not to trap any air bubbles or blisters. If you foul it up by getting things misaligned, you can peel off the laminate by prying up one corner slightly and squishing in cement solvent with an ear syringe, gradually pulling the laminate up as you go along. It's tedious and messy. So do the job right in the first place.

Epoxy glue is made in many forms by many manufacturers. It comes in two parts, both liquid, and is mixed in the required amount just before using. It's a good wood glue and it glues almost anything else, as well. As it's usually 100 per cent solids (no solvent to evaporate), it can be used to stick large areas of metal together. Here solvent-drying glues wouldn't work because the solvent couldn't get out from between the metal surfaces. It's in the high price range even in the small tubes (twin types with one of the liquids in each tube) usually found in hardware and dime stores. It holds with a strength of 1 ton per square inch or more, it doesn't shrink, it's completely waterproof, heat doesn't soften it, and it doesn't creep or slide under steady loads. So it's a good choice for problem jobs like sticking a metal towel rack to a tiled bathroom wall.

Hide glue, now available mainly through cabinetmaker's supply houses, is the traditional woodworking glue of the old time craftsman. It's made in flake, strip, and liquid form, and the price varies accordingly, from low to medium high. It's not waterproof, is weakened by dampness, but it's stronger than most woods, and is a good, easy-to-use gap-filler type. If you decide to use any, ask for full instructions where you buy it, as the flake and strip forms must be soaked in just the right amount of water, then heated, and applied and clamped before cooling.

Buna-N adhesive, like Pliobond, has a base of Buna-N synthetic rubber, is light beige in color, sticks just about anything to anything (so long as the solvent can escape), and dries so flexible it's used to hold pockets and patches in overalls. Don't use this to patch a tire, as rubber cement made for the purpose is better. But use this type of adhesive to patch ripped rugs, work clothes, and anything else that calls for flexible glue. And use it to stick unlike materials together, as in fastening rubber gasket stripping to a vitreous-enameled refrigerator. This isn't a wood glue, though it will stick to wood if it's to hold something that can't be held otherwise. As to strength, one of its original purposes was that of holding the aluminum skin to pursuit plane rudders that were too thin to be riveted.

Polyester resin glue, made by many manufacturers, is the type that holds fiberglass boats together. It comes in the form of two liquids that are mixed before using, and it smells like escaping illuminating or stove gas. The liquid in the smaller of the two containers is a highly flammable peroxide that has to be kept well away from any flame. But when the mixed glue hardens, the fire hazard fades, so a fiberglass boat doesn't burn any faster than plywood. Special forms of this glue, like the Vermont Marble Company's Marfix are designed for the repair of such things as cracked marble table tops. This, and conventional types, can be pigmented to match the material they're repairing. Protect your eyes when you use this glue, and make a small test batch to be sure the mixing proportions on the container are correct for the drying time you need. An error here (and there have been a few) can result in the glue hardening in the middle of the job—which may spell disaster.

Polyvinyl resin glue, like Elmer's Glue-All, is the white glue sold just about everywhere in plastic squeeze bottles. It's ready to use, easy to use, strong, and a good gap-filler in joints that don't fit too snugly. But it isn't waterproof and it can be softened by excessive heat. And it may creep a little under some conditions with a steady, heavy load. So use it where the joint, itself, takes the major load, and the glue's job is simply that of holding the joint together. (This is the usual furniture-type joint.) Although it's white when you apply it, you'll find it transparent when dry, so it eliminates many fix-it job finish problems. On light joints it's stiff enough for moderate handling after about half an hour, fully hardened after about seventy-two hours. It's in the low to middling price range, and a good general purpose wood fix-it glue. But don't use it in contact with metal, as it has corrosive properties.

Resorcinol resin glue, like Elmer's Boat Glue, is a two-part type that's sold in double cans. One can contains a wine-colored liquid, the other a powder. Protect your eyes when you do the mixing as the flour-fine powder can be puffed into the air easily, and can be very injurious. This is the glue developed to hold torpedo boats together, so it's ideal for outdoor furniture and pleasure boats. It's completely waterproof when it hardens, but while still liquid (even after mixing the two parts) it can be washed off brushes and mixing bowls with plain cold water. At average temperatures you have about an hour's working time after mixing. It sets hard in about eight hours at around 70 degrees. Pricewise, it's in the medium high range at about the same general level as top-quality paint.

Rubber base adhesive, like Miracle Adhesive, is in the medium price range, and sticks just about anything to anything, like the Buna-N type, but it sets hard instead of flexible. It's usually black in color but it takes paint nicely after it's *thoroughly* hard—but don't brush the paint on too heavily in the first coat. This adhesive is widely used in sticking metal letters to polished-stone building fronts, and it can do a nice job of holding things to ceramic tile bathroom walls. It also does a fine job of locking nuts on bolts where vibration is likely to cause loosening. (Handy on your car.) And for boating fans, it has a hard-to-match ability. It will stick to the wet, slimy bottom of a boat to caulk a seam under water—and stay there for the rest of the season. Just don't use it where gasoline or oil can get at it, as either one can soften it. As to strength and sealing power, it's not a wood glue (though it can be used to stick other materials to wood.) But it blocks water so well it has often been used to stick a cofferdam to the side of a seagoing ship to let welders work in an open-air compartment well below the waterline.

Trichloroethylene cement, like Styroweld, is formulated with the same solvent used in cleaning fluids like Carbona (Styroweld is made by the same company), and actually fuses styrene-type plastics together. If you apply the cement to the broken edge of a styrene plastic refrigerator food container, for example, the trichloroethylene dissolves the plastic and enables it to blend with similar plastic in the cement. Do this to both edges of a broken section of plastic, press them together, and the break actually fuses into a single piece, as in its original form. While this cement is ineffective on many other types of plastic, it is ideal for the styrene materials widely used for kitchen items and for hobby kits. To determine if an item is made of styrene-type plastic, just touch a dab of the cement on any part of the plastic surface. If that spot softens and blends with the cement you know it's the right type. The cement is inexpensive, sold in ready-to-use tubes.

CLAMPS—TYPES AND USES

Clamps are used to hold glued surfaces in contact until the glue hardens. How long the clamps must remain in place depends on the type of glue and the type of work. In many cases no actual clamping is necessary. Aliphatic resin glue, for example, becomes firm so quickly that many light parts may be hand-held in position long enough (several minutes) for the glue to stiffen sufficiently. In the case of cellulose nitrate cement used on porous wood, still another handy factor is present. This cement shrinks as it dries, actually drawing the parts together in an automatically tightened joint. The gap-filling qualities of many of the other common wood glues, such as casein, resorcinol, and the all-purpose acrylics, also make clamping less critical.

How tight is right?

When you tighten any type of gluing clamp, you squeeze the glue layer between the joining parts and some of the glue oozes out of the seam. If you tighten the clamps too much, you can actually squeeze out almost all of the glue so that you produce a weak joint. In industrial gluing, the clamping pressure can be regulated according to the required pounds per square inch. On a home job, however, you'll just have to get the feel of it. The best method: coat two scrap pieces of wood with the glue you'll be using and clamp them together. Then release the clamps, separate the pieces, and examine the gluing surfaces. If you have squeezed out almost all the glue, your clamps were too tight. If there still remains a glue film on the gluing surfaces, you've done the job right. So tighten your clamps accordingly on the job that counts.

What kind of clamps?

The C-clamp is the commonest general purpose clamp. It gets its name from its shape. You can buy this type in a wide variety of sizes in dime stores and hardware stores at prices that vary with the maximum thickness that can be held in them. They're handy for a wide range of glue jobs but, as the jaws are metal, small pads of scrap wood should be used between the jaws and the work being clamped in order to avoid clamping marks.

Hand clamps are a traditional wooden type long used in cabinetwork and general woodworking. These have wooden jaws that can be adjusted with twin clamping screws to apply pressure to either parallel or angled surfaces. Although these cost more than C-clamps of equivalent size, they have a wider range of uses. And they don't require pads.

The bar clamp has one jaw fixed at the end of a flat metal bar, the other jaw (with the screw clamp in it) adjustable to any position along the bar. This is the type you need when clamping pressure has to be applied across considerable distance, as across the front or top of a cabinet. A variation of this type uses ordinary pipe for the bar, making an extension to almost any reasonable length inexpensive. When only a single clamping job is to be done, however, you can often make your own version of a bar clamp. Simply use a piece of 2 x 4 lumber a little longer than the clamping distance. Nail a block to the face of the lumber at each end, so the inner ends of the blocks are slightly farther apart than the surfaces to be clamped. Then hold the entire unit on the work in such a position that you can tap a wooden wedge between one of the blocks and the work, drawing the block at the other end

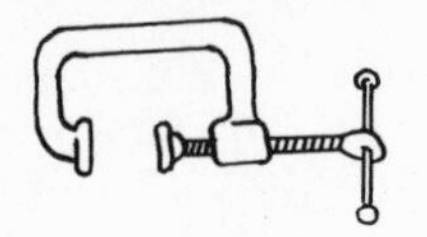

The C-clamp, commonest workshop clamp, is the best choice for general gluing.

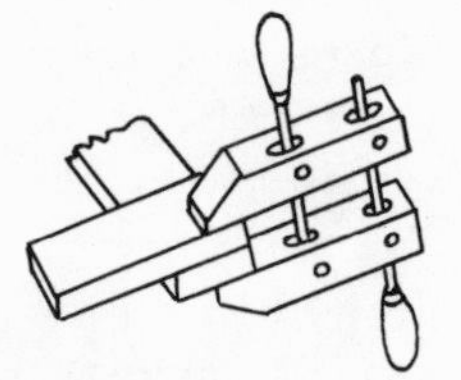

The hand clamp is in the high price bracket, can be adjusted to hold parts at wide range of angles. It's handy for complex jobs.

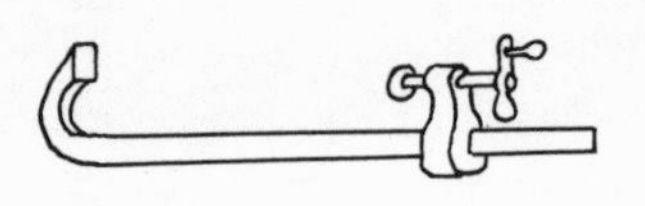

The bar clamp can be adjusted to fit wide work like table tops. Slide the adjustable section to the desired position and tighten it. It locks automatically in most types.

tightly against the work. This provides ample clamping pressure for most jobs.

The band clamp is basically a canvas strap with a bucklelike arrangement that lets you draw it tight around something, and then tighten it still more with a thumbscrew. This is the type you need for clamping irregular shapes like hexagons.

The corner clamp consists of two deep-notched pieces and a threaded rod or other adjustable connection between them. You might use two of these units to glue the corners of a large picture frame. You'd set the notched parts on the corners, crisscross the connecting members diagonally across the frame, and tighten the clamps. This would squeeze the corners together for a firm glue-clamping job.

The band, or strap clamp wraps around work, can be used to hold round assemblies, hexagonals, and so forth.

The spring clamp is very much like an overgrown spring-type clothespin or a pair of pliers with a spring to close the jaws. Just

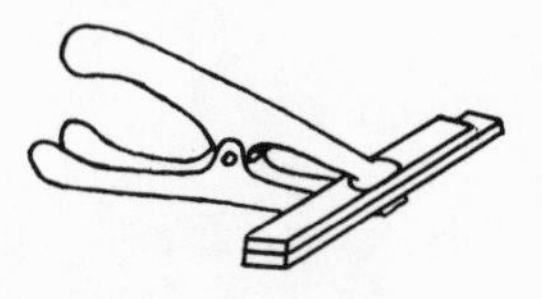

Spring clamp works like an overgrown spring clothespin. Use it for light work.

squeeze the handles together to open the jaws, slip the jaws over the parts to be clamped, and release the handles. The jaws close with enough pressure for light work.

Substitutes for clamps

Even when some clamping pressure is required, it's often possible to provide it without any true clamps. In many cases you can nail the parts together temporarily with some provision for removing the nails after the glue sets. (You can use form nails if the nail holes won't show—otherwise use finishing nails with scrap wood blocks under their heads.) For light pressure you can use weights of a type to suit the job. These may range from old books to jars of water or bricks. If there's any chance of the weight being accidentally glued to the work, cover the weighted area with several layers of tissue paper before applying the weights.

Rubber bands often come in handy for clamping light work, too. If you can put the rubber band all the way around the work, it's easy. Wipe off squeezed-out glue where it touches the rubber band. This makes it easy to get the rubber off. If you can't stretch the rubber band all the way around the work, you can often use an ordinary pair of pliers as a spring clamp. Just close the plier jaws against the work so as to clamp it, and stretch rubber bands across the plier handles to maintain the pressure after you let go of the pliers.

Twisted cord is another widely used substitute for clamps, especially in gluing furniture rungs. After the rungs have been glue-coated and fitted into the holes in the furniture legs, cord is looped tightly around each pair of legs involved, tied securely, and twisted by means of a short stick for further tightening.

HOW TO MOUNT A SHELF

Mounting a shelf on the wall calls for locating at least two studs inside the wall. You do it by the same method used in heavy-picture hanging, but you do it at the height where you want to mount the shelf. Then you mount standard shelf brackets from the hardware store, in a size to match the width of the shelf you plan to use. First, hold them up on the wall at the position already measured up from the floor, and directly over the studs.

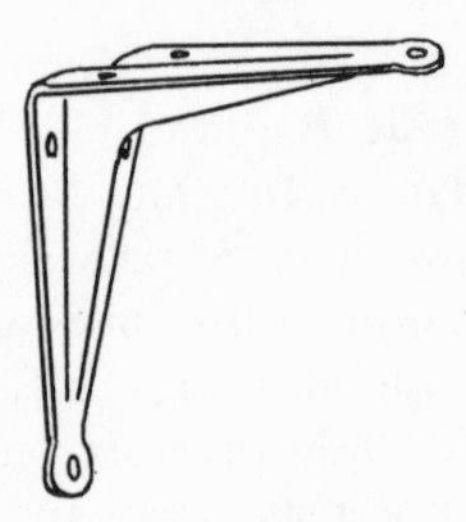

Shelf brackets like this are available in various forms, some more ornamental than this. Screw the vertical part into studs.

Pencil-mark through the screw holes in each bracket, then put the brackets aside. Use an awl, ice pick, or push drill to drill through the wall into the stud at each pencil mark. Then use 1¼-inch or 1½-inch screws (of a diameter to fit the holes in the brackets) to mount the brackets on the wall. Place the wooden shelf on top of the brackets, slide it to the right position, snug against the wall, and drive shorter screws up into it through the bracket holes. The screws must not be so long they poke through the top of the shelf. That's all there is to it. Some people fasten the brackets to the shelf first, then mount the whole business on the wall. This makes the job a little easier, but increases the risk of mislocating the brackets in relation to the studs.

BUILDING A BOOKCASE FITTED TO YOUR BOOKS

Making a set of bookshelves is really a furniture-building job, and a good one for a beginner. Start by measuring the depth of your books in the position they'll occupy on the shelves. Then buy your lumber accordingly. For most books, nominal 1 x 8 square-edge number 1 board grade pine does the trick—if the span between supports isn't greater than about 30 inches. (For the popular encyclopedias, you'll need 1 x 10 lumber.) If the span

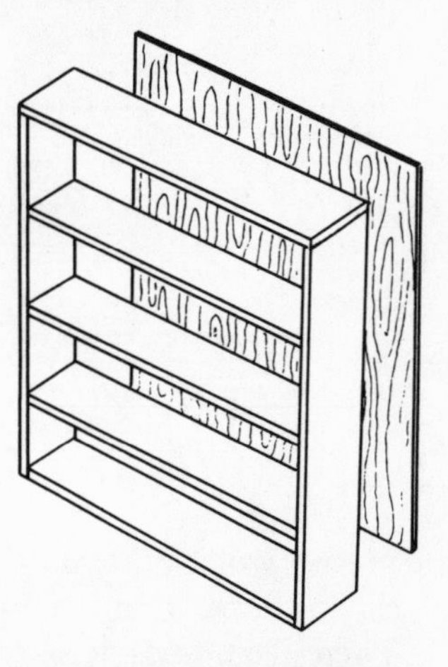

If you build a bookcase, always use a back panel, as shown. This keeps the unit from skewing to one side or the other. The unit shown has the simplest type of shelf-end joints.

must be greater, say around 4 feet, switch to nominal 2-inch lumber. You can either make the vertical supports for the shelves as shown in the drawings or buy metal ones ready-made at the hardware store or lumberyard. The choice depends to a considerable extent on the décor of the room. The metal supports sometimes clash with traditional furnishings.

If you are using wooden verticals at the ends of your shelves, you want to be sure that the nails you drive into the ends of the shelves actually go into the shelf ends, not just below or just above them. If the construction is the simplest type shown in the drawing, you should first draw pencil lines on the *inside* of the vertical end pieces showing the position of the upper and lower surfaces of each shelf. These lines will, of course, be parallel, with a space between them equal to the thickness of the shelf. To make sure your nails, driven from the outside of the vertical end

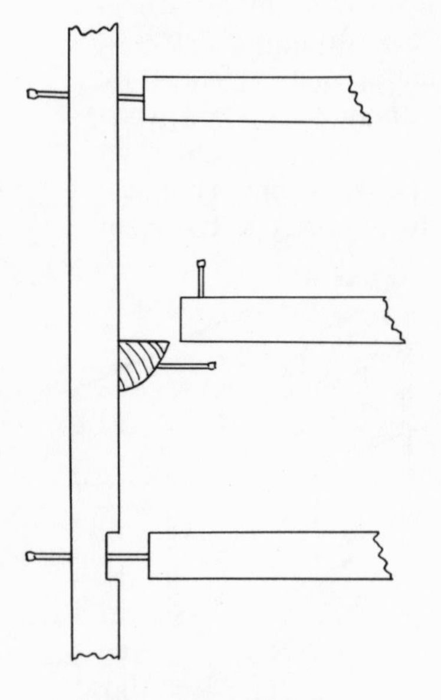

Three ways to mount shelf ends in a shelf unit like a bookcase. You can simply nail them (as at top) if you hate work. You can use sections of quarter-round ¾-inch molding as cleats under the ends. Or you can notch the side member about one quarter to three eighths of an inch to take the shelf ends. To make the notches, first make a saw cut at each outer limit of the notch. Then make close-together cuts between them. You can click out the wood between the close-together cuts. Then smooth out the notch with a chisel.

pieces, won't miss, do this: make pencil lines across the edge of the verticals from the ends of the inner lines to the outer surface. Then make lines across the outer surface exactly matching those on the inside. If you drive your nails between these lines (and drive them straight), they'll go directly into the ends of the shelves. Use a try square to get all these lines perpendicular to surfaces and edges (see Chapter 2), and make your pencil lines light if you plan a natural finish. It's easy to sand off a light pencil line but not a heavy one.

One important feature of a set of bookshelves is a back panel.

This may not seem necessary, as the wall is behind the shelves anyway. But the back panel adds greatly to the strength of the unit by preventing it from skewing to one side or the other under the load of the books. You can make the back panel either from ¼-inch plywood or hardboard like Masonite. Nail it to all parts.

If you plan to make other pieces of furniture, your best construction guide is other furniture. Unpainted furniture on display is usually a good example of simple basic construction. Early American antiques are another excellent guide. These are simply constructed because only simple tools were used to make the originals. And if you do the job the same way and add an authentic bit of wood-distressing here and there, you may end up with something that looks enough like the real thing to fool most people.

For lavish touches, get a catalogue from a cabinetmaker's supply house like Albert Constantine and Son, of New York. These places can supply such things as ready-made carvings, carved legs, antique hardware replicas, and assorted inlays, as well as rare woods and veneers. You're not likely to have the equipment you need for all-out veneer work, but some of the edgings are a cinch for anybody to use.

WHERE DO YOU GO FROM HERE?

When you've reached the stage of handymanning when you're actually building attractive things for your home, you're not really a handyman any more. Certainly you're not an Awful Handyman. Maybe you're a designer or builder. Maybe you have a fancier name for it. In any event, there's no telling how far you'll go with your tool kit, and a few examples of what other nonprofessionals have done may trigger something beyond your wildest dreams.

First, realize that you belong to an enormous band of spenders. Home handymen and similar souls who consider themselves amateurs pay around *four billion dollars a year* for their tools and materials. And to say the least, they do some amazing things. In a sample suburban area, for example, a list of people who built their own houses from the ground up, with their own hands, included a concert pianist, a police detective, a commercial artist, an airline pilot, a butler, a machinist, a retired colonel, and the author of this book. Quite a few had never built even a doghouse before. How good was their work? Today, about fifteen years later, all the homes are in tip-top shape. One was sold for nearly $70,000, another for more than $30,000. And the butler liked the new line of work so much he switched to the building business and later retired, financially independent. And that's not all. Many a young buck with a longing to fly has built his own plane and taken to the skies in it—even in the past year. And other speed-minded folks have built outboard racers in apartments and smuggled them down on freight elevators at three in the morning. There's the true story of the newlyweds who passed up a honeymoon to build a cabin sloop—and took off in it on their first sailboat ride. They sailed it for ten years and then built a bigger one. There's also the true story of the retired newspaper art director who liked sailing. With leisure time on his hands, he casually turned out one of the fastest racing sailers in the world.

Right now, if you merely want to fix things around the house, you may not think you'll ever get around to the kind of performances just described. But don't bank on it. One of the best-known producers of do-it-yourself patterns never had a hammer in his hand until the refrigerator in his historic country home fell through the floor. When he fixed the floor, he found to his surprise, that tool work is easy. And the name of the company he founded, Easi-Bild, still emphasizes the point.

This has been going on for generations, and when you play around with tools, you never know if your turn is next. If you ever think about building your house, you may go down to the hardware store to see a framing square, for example. You need one of these things when you get into house-building. And it's a cheerful tool. The hard-working blacksmith who made the first one in his scant spare time more than 150 years ago found it was so popular he had to give up blacksmithing to make more of them. And a few years later, with a string of factories turning out his handiwork, he decided to quit working altogether, and retired in comfort and wealth. So when you start out to be a handyman, awful or otherwise, never underestimate the possibilities.

INDEX

INDEX

INDEX

INDEX

INDEX

INDEX

GEORGE DANIELS has, among other things, designed and built (out of native lumber cut from logs and processed at a local sawmill) his own seven-room, two-bath house from the ground up, including the plumbing and wiring. He has also designed and built the furniture in it, twenty-two boats, from a large motor yacht to an all-glued canoe with no nails or screws, two sports cars, and a glider.

Most of this work was done in connection with a book or magazine article Mr. Daniels was writing. He began his career at the age of fifteen, when his first article—on model plane design—appeared in *Aero Digest*. He later became a newspaper reporter and then aviation editor of *Mechanix Illustrated*. After serving in World War II Mr. Daniels gave up flying and concentrated on the burgeoning do-it-yourself trend. He headed the do-it-yourself department for Fawcett Publications, then for *Science Illustrated*.

Mr. Daniels is now a free-lance writer. He is the author of eight books and hundreds of magazine articles for such publications as *House & Garden*, *Better Homes & Gardens*, *Popular Science*, *Mechanix Illustrated*, *Popular Photography*, and many others. He lives in Danbury with his wife, also a writer and former journalist, who works with him on most of his building projects.